The Origins of French Absolutism, 1598–1661

SEMINAR STUDIES IN HISTORY

The Origins of French Absolutism, 1598–1661

ALAN JAMES

PEARSON
Longman

Harlow, England • London • New York • Boston • San Francisco • Toronto
Sydney • Tokyo • Singapore • Hong Kong • Seoul • Taipei • New Delhi
Cape Town • Madrid • Mexico City • Amsterdam • Munich • Paris • Milan

PEARSON EDUCATION LIMITED

Edinburgh Gate
Harlow CM20 2JE
United Kingdom
Tel: +44 (0)1279 623623
Fax: +44 (0)1279 431059
Website: www.pearsoned.co.uk

First edition published in Great Britain in 2006

© Pearson Education Limited 2006

The right of Alan James to be identified as author
of this work has been asserted by him in accordance
with the Copyright, Designs and Patents Act 1988.

ISBN-13: 978-0-582-36900-9
ISBN-10: 0-582-36900-2

British Library Cataloguing in Publication Data
A CIP catalogue record for this book can be obtained from the British Library

Library of Congress Cataloging in Publication Data
James, Alan, 1965–
   The origins of French absolutism, 1598–1661 / Alan James.—1st ed.
      p. cm. — (Seminar studies in history)
   Includes bibliographical references and index.
   ISBN-13: 978-0-582-36900-9 (alk. paper)
   ISBN-10: 0-582-36900-2 (alk. paper)
      1. France—Politics and government—17th century. 2. Monarchy—France—History—17th
century. 3. Fronde. 4. Nobility—France—History. 5. Religion—France—History—17th
century. 6. Government, Resistance to—France—History—17th century. 7.
France—History—17th century. I. Title. II. Series.

   JN2341.J36 2006
   944′.032—dc22
                                                                                    2005055585

Cover illustration: The Majority of Louis XIII (1601–43), 20th October 1614, (oil on canvas)
by Peter Paul Rubens (1577–1640) © Musée de Louvre, Paris, France/Bridgeman Art Library,
London.

10 9 8 7 6 5 4 3 2 1
10 09 08 07 06

Set by 35 in 10/12.5pt Sabon
Printed and bound in Malaysia

The Publisher's policy is to use paper manufactured from sustainable forests.

FOR ROBERT AND WILLIAM

CONTENTS

INTRODUCTION TO THE SERIES

Such is the pace of historical enquiry in the modern world that there is an ever-widening gap between the specialist article or monograph, incorporating the results of current research, and general surveys, which inevitably become out of date. *Seminar Studies in History* is designed to bridge this gap. The series was founded by Patrick Richardson in 1966 and his aim was to cover major themes in British, European and World history. Between 1980 and 1996 Roger Lockyer continued his work, before handing the editorship over to Clive Emsley and Gordon Martel. Clive Emsley is Professor of History at the Open University, while Gordon Martel is Professor of International History at the University of Northern British Columbia, Canada, and Senior Research Fellow at De Montfort University.

All the books are written by experts in their field who are not only familiar with the latest research but have often contributed to it. They are frequently revised, in order to take account of new information and interpretations. They provide a selection of documents to illustrate major themes and provoke discussion, and also a guide to further reading. The aim of *Seminar Studies in History* is to clarify complex issues without over-simplifying them, and to stimulate readers into deepening their knowledge and understanding of major themes and topics.

ACKNOWLEDGEMENTS

We are grateful to the following for permission to reproduce copyright material:
Map of France in 1620 reproduced with permission from D. Lublinskaya,
French Absolutism: The Crucial Phase, 1620–1629, Cambridge University
Press, 1968.

In some instances we have been unable to trace the owners of copyright
material, and we would appreciate any information that would enable us to
do so.

CHRONOLOGY

1598	13 April, promulgation of the Edict of Nantes; 13 May, Peace of Vervins with Spain
1600	17 December, marriage of Henri IV and Marie de Medici
1601	27 December, birth of the future Louis XIII
1602	31 July, execution of Marshal Biron for rebellion
1603	Jesuits reintroduced to France
1604	Establishment of the Carmelites in France
1605	Sully's pre-eminence on the royal council secured
1606	Rebellion led by Duke of Bouillon put down
1610	14 May, assassination of Henri IV. Start of the reign of Louis XIII and the regency government of his mother Marie de Medici. 17 October, coronation of Louis XIII
1611	French Oratory established for training priests
1612	Establishment of the Ursulines in France. Sully removed from office
1614	Condé in rebellion. October, opening of the meeting of the Estates-General (which ended in 1615). Majority of Louis XIII declared
1615	Rebellion led by Condé; 25 November, marriage of Louis XIII and Anne of Austria
1616	1 September, Condé arrested leading to further noble rebellion. Richelieu briefly joined the royal council as a client of Queen Mother
1617	24 April, murder of the Queen Mother's favourite, Concini. Luynes replaced him as principal minister
1618	Outbreak of Thirty Years' War in German Empire
1619	Richelieu helped to negotiate the end of the fighting between Louis XIII and Marie de Medici
1620–22	First of the seventeenth-century wars against Huguenots
1620	Noble rebellion resumed. 7 August, Louis XIII victorious at the Ponts-de-Cé against those loyal to Marie de Medici. 19 October, reunion of Béarn to France. December, assembly at La Rochelle put Huguenots on war footing

1621	Successful campaign against the Huguenots stalled with the failure of the siege of Montauban in November, followed by the death of Luynes
1622	18 October, Peace of Montpellier ended first war with the Huguenots; Richelieu became a cardinal
1624	April, Richelieu rejoined the royal council. November, French fighting papal troops for control of the Valtelline, a strategic Swiss alpine pass
1625–26	Second war against the Huguenots, ended with a naval victory in September over La Rochelle
1625	Establishment of the Lazarists by Vincent de Paul
1626	Richelieu secured his pre-eminence on the council. Became Grand-Master of Navigation, established a number of trading companies; Chalais conspiracy to kill Richelieu failed
1627–29	Third war against the Huguenots
1627	September, beginning of the siege of La Rochelle. 8 November, defeat of English forces under the Duke of Buckingham which had been supporting the Huguenots. Execution of Montmorency-Boutteville for defying a ban on duelling
1628	28 October, Louis XIII and Richelieu entered the starving city of La Rochelle after royal victory
1629	28 June, Peace of Alès with the Huguenots ends fighting in the south. French forces in northern Italy raised the siege of Casale in support of the Duke of Nevers' claims to be Duke of Mantua
1630	10 November, Day of the Dupes in which Louis XIII backed Richelieu against his detractors who now included Marie de Medici and Gaston d'Orléans. French forces took Pinerolo
1631	Treaty with Spain secured Nevers as Duke of Mantua. Marie de Medici and Gaston d'Orléans left France
1632	Gaston d'Orléans secretly married daughter of the Duke of Lorraine, then aided the Duke of Montmorency in rebellion in the south of France. Montmorency was executed; Gaston went into exile again
1633	French occupation of Lorraine. Daughters of Charity founded
1634–35	Widespread introduction of *intendants*
1635	February, foundation of the Académie Française. 19 May, France declared war against Spain. The start of the 'Croquants' rebellion in the south-west including disturbances in Bordeaux
1636	The 'Year of Corbie'. 15 August, Spanish forces entered the north of France within eighty miles of Paris

1637	'Croquants' rebellion spread
1638	10 January, Louis XIII dedicated his reign to the Virgin Mary. 8 September, birth of the future Louis XIV. Arrest of the Jansenist Abbot of Saint-Cyran. Unsuccessful French siege on the Basque port of Fuenterrabia
1639	Start of the '*nu-pieds*' rebellion in Normandy
1640	Rebellions against Spanish crown in Catalonia and Portugal helped French war effort
1641	15 December, Mazarin became a cardinal
1642	Chapel at the Sorbonne completed. Death of Marie de Medici. 4 December, death of Richelieu. Mazarin joined the royal council
1643	14 May, death of Louis XIII and start of the regency government of Anne of Austria for the young Louis XIV. 19 May, French victory at Rocroi under Condé
1644	French victories led to peace talks in Westphalia
1645	Start of the construction of the Val-de-Grâce church by Anne of Austria
1647	Appointment of Italian, Particelli d'Emery, as Superintendent of Finance caused upset
1648	29 April, meeting of representatives of the courts in the *Chambre St Louis* opened the Fronde. Particelli d'Emery dismissed. Abolition of most *intendants*. 20 August, Condé victorious against the Spanish at Lens. Arrest of leading parlementarians led to barricades in the streets of Paris, 26–28 August. 24 October, Peace of Westphalia ended the war in the German empire and between Spain and the United Provinces. Disorder in the provinces and in Paris. Royal Academy of Painting founded with Mazarin as protector
1649	Royal family in exile. Condé led a royal army to take Paris from frondeurs; 12 March, Peace of Rueil ended this phase of the Fronde with many concessions by the crown to the demands of the office-holders; collapse of royal authority in the provinces. Royal court returned to Paris
1650	18 January, arrest of Condé, Conti and Longueville; the Fronde of the Nobles began. October, Louis XIV and Anne of Austria entered Bordeaux
1651	13 February, increasing tension led to the release of Condé and the other prince; Mazarin forced into temporary exile; 7 September, majority of Louis XIV declared. Condé returned to Bordeaux for support
1652	April, Condé headed a rebel army against Paris; July, defeated by Turenne; August, Mazarin voluntarily returned into exile

	to undercut opposition; 14 October, unsuccessful Condé now in exile. 21 October, Louis XIV returned to Paris. 19 December, Retz arrested. Val-de-Grâce completed
1653	February, Mazarin returned to office; 31 July, capitulation of Bordeaux ending the Fronde in the provinces. Pope Innocent X declared Jansenist teaching to be heretical
1654	7 June, coronation of Louis XIV at Reims
1655	13 April, Louis XIV forbade parlement from interfering in government
1658	14 June, Turenne's victory at the Battle of the Dunes ended Condé's campaigns against France in alliance with Spain
1659	7 November, Peace of the Pyrenees between France and Spain
1660	January, army under Louis XIV took rebellious Marseille; 9 June, marriage of Louis XIV and Maria-Theresa of Spain; Condé pardoned for his part in the Fronde
1661	9 March, death of Mazarin. Louis XIV announced his intention to rule without a first minister. 5 September, Fouquet arrested; Colbert given authority over finances. 1 November, birth of the Dauphin, heir to the throne. French clergy ordered to condemn Jansenism

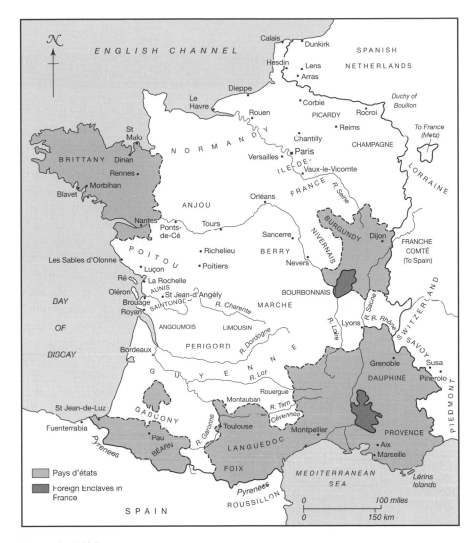

France in 1620

INTRODUCTION

The seventeenth century was the *grand siècle*, or golden age, of French history. With a population of approximately 20 million, France was the largest country in Europe, with human and material resources that gave it a clear advantage over its neighbours. This was an age of great ambition and of increased effectiveness and authority for the monarchy. It was also an age of long, costly wars whose legacy was decidedly mixed. French military victories were often matched by equally significant setbacks. The scale of the fighting put enormous strain on the government's ability to cope and on the population's willingness and ability to pay for it. Nevertheless, through its wars, France gradually established its military pre-eminence. With this status came an equal cultural pre-eminence, not just in the arts but also in political style and manners. The architectural magnificence of the palace and gardens of Versailles, and the elaborate courtly rituals conducted therein, served as a model throughout Europe. The court of the Sun King, Louis XIV, the monarch who was the living symbol of France's greatness, was housed there from 1682. He fashioned himself as the embodiment of all of France's achievements, including its growing government and complex system of political relations of power which came later to be known to historians simply as royal 'absolutism'.

An observer from the late sixteenth century would have had difficulty predicting such developments. France at the time was mired in a long, costly civil war. The confessional tension between Protestants and Catholics and the physical destructiveness of the 'Wars of Religion' (1562–98) were as damaging to the economy and to local communities as they were to the authority of the crown. Historians often credit Henri IV (1589–1610), the first of the Bourbon monarchs, with bringing an end to the troubles by promulgating the celebrated Edict of Nantes of 1598 which protected the Huguenots, as the French Protestant (or, more specifically, Calvinist) minority was called. With peace came the reassertion of royal authority and the development of more effective government. In 1624, Cardinal Richelieu joined the royal council and has been celebrated for taking the process much further. Made famous in the popular imagination by the novelist Alexandre Dumas as the jealous, authoritarian evil-genius behind the weak figure of the new king, Louis XIII (1610–43), Richelieu has also been the object of generations of historians' scholarly interest. His achievements in government have been scrutinised exceptionally closely to reveal, more accurately, an effective administrator, minister of state, and servant to the king. Richelieu nevertheless retains his reputation among historians for ruthlessness, extraordinary political strength and formidable will, all of which were put to the service of the state. For insisting on the enforcement of the royal will, he is sometimes considered the principal architect of French absolutism. As a cardinal of the Catholic Church, his ministry is also noteworthy for the seemingly inappropriate military support offered to Protestant princes abroad and for formally taking France into the Thirty Years' War in 1635. This war, fought chiefly against Catholic Spain, lasted until 1659. It was fought on an unprecedented scale, and it is difficult to overstate its impact on French society. As for Richelieu, his apparently anti-Catholic foreign policy has earned him a reputation as the first secular statesman, motivated by reason, pragmatism, and the interests of the state alone (Church, 1972).

After Richelieu's death in December 1642 and that of Louis XIII in May 1643, France went through a tremendously difficult period of readjustment in the form of a series of rebellions against the government from 1648 to 1653, known collectively as the Fronde. The anger in French society, which the Fronde so eloquently and violently expressed, was directed against the government of Cardinal Mazarin, Richelieu's successor as principal minister to the new king, Louis XIV (1643–1715). Whereas England suffered the traumas of the Civil War, the French monarchy survived its nearly contemporaneous troubles with its power reinforced. Thus, Mazarin not only inherited his political position from Richelieu, but he shares his historical reputation as a founding father of French absolutism. In the aftermath of the Fronde, Louis XIV imposed his authority over the rebels, who came from all walks of society, and in this sense the Fronde acted as a springboard to the illustrious reign that followed. When Mazarin died in 1661, Louis XIV chose not to replace him as principal minister. Henceforth, the king would take responsibility for all aspects of government himself. With this decision, a new era in French government is said to have opened. The final obstacles to the absolutism begun by Henri IV seem to have been lifted, and his grandson, the energetic, ambitious Louis XIV was set to take full advantage.

The term absolutism was coined in the eighteenth century to describe Louis XIV's reign, and it was popular in the nineteenth century with historians seeking to provide inspiration to a nation shaken by internal upheaval from 1848 or battered by foreign armies in the 1870s. The twentieth century, too, has seen many historians actively seeking in the past the sources of the nation's strength and celebrating the heroes who built the modern French state. Perhaps not surprisingly, a fundamental shift away from this approach has developed among historians. Indeed, over the last half century there has been a determined effort to peer behind the facade of royal grandeur to expose the incoherence and weaknesses of government. The trend for many today is to see the *Louis Quatorzien* court as a carefully choreographed display, a political construction which served to enhance the king's image and his reputation and, thereby, shore up his practical authority (Burke, 'Fabrication', 1992). By far the greatest number of works on seventeenth-century French history of the late twentieth and early twenty-first centuries has stressed the limits of the king's real power, calling into question the validity of absolutism as an historical model. Detailed studies of various aspects of the reign suggest that absolutism was always more theoretical than real. The crown was never in a position to rule without regard for the existing institutions of power, various corporate bodies or the influence of established elites. Louis XIV's success seems to have been based less on his own unlimited power and more on the creation of an image of greatness, while carefully balancing competing interests within his kingdom. Indeed, one historian has argued that the notion of absolute power has become so thoroughly discredited that we should dispense with the term absolutism altogether (Henshall, 1992).

Accordingly, there has been a similar shift in our understanding of the formative years 1598–1661 and of the reputations of the two most high-profile political figures of the period: the cardinals Richelieu and Mazarin. Though they still dominate the political landscape of the time, they are no longer held in exaggerated esteem as the self-conscious creators of the modern, centralised state. Their careers can be recounted instead as a series of failed, grand designs and compromises. Or, more sympathetically (and most recently), they are seen as skilful and careful politicians, subject to all of the demands and dangers of the time. Though their influence was enormous, they actually seem to have been driven much less by any ideological agenda than by the quotidian pressures of the increasing scale of international warfare and of internal rebellion. They dealt with situations as they arose, imperfectly and with mixed results. This process, of establishing the 'myth' of absolutism and of revealing the complexities and ambiguities of political power, has been extremely useful. Undoubtedly, we now have a much more measured and sensitive understanding of the workings of government and of the nature of the French state. The government was much less powerful than once thought. Its authority was severely circumscribed, and its exercise throughout the seventeenth century was often blunt and brutal, not the fruit of progressive institutional reform (Mettam, 1988).

Nevertheless, there is still an inescapable progression. In 1598, France emerged exhausted from nearly forty years of upheaval and religious and civil war. By 1661, Louis XIV was embarking on his so-called period of 'personal rule', with unprecedented military and political power at his disposal. The monarchy was clearly much stronger in the 1660s than in the 1590s, and greater institutional control and an expanded bureaucracy is the clearest evidence of this. Yet to focus attention on the nature and extent of these changes, that is to say on the mechanics and structure of government, as historians are so often tempted to do, is to risk overlooking its broader purpose. In other words, reflecting too exclusively on 'how' government operated, rather than 'why', opens one to the danger of missing its more significant failures and, especially, its successes. Whatever might be said about changes in the style of government under Henri IV, for example, his actions reveal long-established, traditional priorities. As king of France, he inherited a profound sense of religious duty, a personal responsibility for fighting just wars, and a deep-seated concern about the strength of his dynasty and his relationship with the rest of the nobility upon which his practical authority ultimately depended. The details of government were simply incidental means to bigger ends defined by these priorities. In this way, he differed in no appreciable way from his predecessors, the Valois kings of France, or from his Bourbon descendants. Thus these three themes of religion, war, and social order (built around the privileged position of the nobility in society) still largely defined the fundamental aims of government in the seventeenth century. They define the focus of the major chapters of this book, for it is only from this perspective that the specific workings of the administration can be assessed properly.

Though we are now intimately aware of the limits of the state's powers and of the compromises and pragmatic deals cut in the process of governing, by adopting this thematic approach and keeping the basic aims of government in sight, it is clear that the six decades following the Edict of Nantes in 1598 were actually most remarkable for the crown's successes, particularly in three climactic years from 1659 to 1661. It is, in fact, not correct to suggest that the origins of French absolutism had been laid in these years, for no such plan ever existed. Nevertheless, something tangible had indeed emerged as a result which shaped, and therefore inevitably defined, the nature of the state that followed. It will be suggested here that this should be measured less by the yardsticks usually associated with absolutism, that is to say by the development, or clever manipulation, of the formal institutions of power, and more by the realisation of the long-held ambitions of the French monarchy. The continuity of aims and methods of government suggests that the radiating brilliance of the reign of the Sun King in the 1660s was less the product of profound structural changes than the effect of a remarkably fortunate and sudden convergence of successes which were most clearly reflected in the overweening confidence with which Louis XIV looked to the future at the outset of his personal rule.

PART ONE　　THE BACKGROUND

CHAPTER ONE

EARLY BOURBON MONARCHY

Henri IV enjoys one of the most favourable reputations of all French monarchs, for his reign is synonymous with the peace and stability brought by the Edict of Nantes of 1598, perhaps the most famous piece of legislation in French history. By enshrining in law a guarantee of freedom of worship for Huguenots in France, the edict has long been celebrated as an early expression of toleration in an intolerant age and for bringing an end to the long, sixteenth-century civil Wars of Religion. The relative peace and stability which followed the edict was indeed the most significant factor in the subsequent recovery of royal authority. Yet there is a danger in seeing in 1598 a sea change in the religious, or political, history of France. It was, rather, merely a step in the 'struggle for stability', as Mark Greengrass refers to the period of Henri IV's reign (Greengrass, 1995).

On occasion during the difficult years of the civil wars, which had raged intermittently since 1562, the French monarchy had been crippled by factional fighting among the nobility and by religious hatred which had brought widespread disorder and suffering to the country at large. Latterly, as the extinction of the Valois line of kings looked likely, the wars were fought specifically over the legitimacy of the succession of the Huguenot Henri of Navarre, the future Henri IV of France, because of his faith. This raised complex constitutional questions and damaged the image of the monarchy. While it is easy to exaggerate the extent to which royal authority had collapsed during the wars, the challenge, nevertheless, would be to confirm the legitimacy of the new dynasty and to restore the prestige of the crown. By 1598, Henri IV had come a long way, yet none of the major problems he faced had been entirely resolved. The religious settlement itself was far less secure than has often been assumed. France still feared foreign intervention, not least from Spain, which was far from indifferent to the prospect of a resurgent France under a strong monarchy. More imminently, perhaps, armed aristocratic rebellion and dangerous political factions remained a serious threat to effective government. These three concerns, therefore, of confessional discord, disruption from Spanish aggression and noble disaffection did not simply belong to a previous era. On the contrary, their resolution was the priority of Henri IV's reign, just as they would drive the subsequent evolution of royal government throughout the seventeenth century.

THE 'PEACE' OF NANTES

The city of Nantes was chosen for the promulgation of the famous edict of the same name because Henri IV was there in 1598 to sign the Peace of Vervins with Spain. He was celebrating the final defeat in Brittany of the lingering, occupying Spanish forces which had supported his enemies within France during the preceding civil wars. Indeed, to contemporary observers, this settlement with Spain was by far the more significant of the two, more likely to bring the stability so badly craved by war-torn France. Unlike Vervins, the Edict of Nantes was clearly the result of military stalemate, only grudgingly accepted by both sides of the confessional divide. In this respect, and in most of its specific terms, it differed little from the many previously unsuccessful and tortuously complex edicts of pacification that had appeared during the wars. In other words, there was nothing intrinsic to this particular settlement which promised to have any greater, or lasting, effect.

Although often credited with allowing freedom of worship, the terms imposed on the Huguenots by the edict were actually very restrictive. Protestant worship was to be allowed wherever it could be proven to have been openly practised in 1596–97. Outside these few privileged areas and the lands of certain Huguenot nobles, however, it was to be restricted to two specific locations within each *bailliage*, or local administrative district, to be chosen by special commissioners of the crown whose purpose was to enforce these terms. In practice, this made life difficult for the Huguenots. Paris was exempt, and many other towns refused to allow 'heretical' worship within their walls. Often Huguenots were forced, therefore, to meet in inconvenient locations at some distance from home. The main body of the edict also made clear that the Huguenots were not allowed any sort of national political assembly. That is to say, they could meet to discuss theological matters in a national synod, but as a group capable of organised political or military action, the Huguenots were to be disbanded [*Doc. 4*].

Apart from this limited freedom of worship and a few other privileges, such as access to public office, the real advantage to the Huguenots as a corporate body came in additional warrants, or *brevets*, that were part of the complex assembly of articles of different legal status that together made up the Edict of Nantes. These *brevets*, however, did not belong in the main body of the theoretically 'irrevocable' edict, and their terms, therefore, were not binding on future kings. They were granted for a limited time and would need periodic renewal to remain valid. According to these concessions, the Huguenots would be allowed some 200 security towns where they could guarantee their physical safety. These could have Protestant governors and would be garrisoned for their defence, about half of them at the crown's expense [*Doc.* 12]. Although in practice even these terms were not always respected and the financial support was slow to arrive, the Huguenots still had a military presence of sorts, especially in the south and west of the country and specifically in their major centres of La Rochelle, Montauban, Sancerre, St Jean-d'Angély and Montpellier.

With the military tension still not entirely resolved and both sides uncomfortable with the religious compromise, one might ask how it was that the Edict of Nantes was so successful at bringing peace. One answer is that the situation now simply seemed impossible to resolve through military force alone, and so a general war-weariness led people to accept it. Yet war-weariness was not new to France in 1598. What made the difference was the extent to which the legal authority of the monarch had been re-established. By this time, Henri IV was in a privileged position to impose a religious settlement and, crucially, to enforce its terms.

On the surface of it, Henri IV seems a most unlikely person to have brought religious peace to France. The succession fell to him in 1589, when the last Valois king, Henri III, died with no direct heir. At the time, he was already king of the largely Protestant, independent principality of Navarre on the southern frontier of France with Spain, and he was the military leader of the Huguenots within France. He had fought, defending the few privileges that the minority enjoyed in an otherwise thoroughly Catholic realm. The Catholic League, which had formed in 1576 to defend Catholic interests, naturally refused to accept the idea of an 'heretical' king of France. In 1593, however, Henri IV undercut the legal and moral basis for opposition to him by publicly renouncing his faith and formally converting to Catholicism, a crucial event which is largely responsible for bringing the wars to an end.

The king's conversion has often been seen as a cynical ploy, and it was undoubtedly a pragmatic move calculated to bring political advantage. Yet there was much more to the consolidation of his authority. Henri IV did not just seize an easy opportunity to secure his throne in this way. He first fought for his legal inheritance. By demonstrating his willingness to fight, and his martial prowess, he had already gone a long way towards establishing his legitimacy as king. Indeed, it seems he had put off earlier chances to convert to Catholicism which would also have been politically expedient (Love, 2001). He did not want just to be a king against whom one no longer had a legal right to rebel, but to be one who commanded active support and respect. The spiritual and the martial were two quintessential elements of early-modern kingship, both of which had to be fostered.

With the king now for all intents and purposes a committed Catholic, many of the Protestant nobles subsequently demonstrated their loyalty in a series of similar conversions. Although Henri IV was more open to having

Huguenots in his service than previous, or indeed subsequent, French kings, there was little left to be gained politically for most people at court from remaining steadfastly and defiantly Protestant. These conversions had a profound effect on the Huguenot church, for the nobility had long been largely responsible for the military strength of the community, providing the resources and leadership necessary to take up arms. As they defected, therefore, the Huguenots became increasingly weak. Yet it was not just this weakness which kept them relatively docile. Rather, it was a recognition that, even though Henri IV had not proven himself to be the champion of Protestantism that they had hoped, their best interests still lay in the meagre terms of the Edict of Nantes and in maintaining the personal, and precarious, goodwill of the king to renew and to enforce them. Implicit in this position is a recognition that a Catholic king of France had the right to impose a religious settlement. Thus, as Philippe Duplessis-Mornay, an influential Huguenot leader and theologian, argued, the Huguenots had to find a way to reconcile their faith with the need for political obedience.

The most high-profile exception to the trend of noble conversions to Catholicism was the Duke of Sully, an old comrade in arms of the king during the civil wars who rose to a position of political pre-eminence in the king's council. Despite entreaties from his royal master, however, Sully always refused to follow his lead and to renounce Protestantism. By refusing to convert, Sully was taking a political risk. For this reason, he could be celebrated for the strength of his faith, unwilling to compromise his convictions for political advantage. While there is undoubtedly merit in this, it could be countered that his favour with the king and his political success was actually already so complete that he simply did not need to convert. Either way, far more than his piety, Sully's actions demonstrate the virtues in this age of personal political loyalty and obedience to the king. He demanded the same principle of loyalty from the Huguenot community to which he maintained close ties. To Sully, and to many other Huguenots who thought the same way, this obedience was the only practical and legitimate basis of survival in the seventeenth century.

Despite the docility of many within the Huguenot community and his own reluctance to be harsh, Henri IV still had to take an active role in implementing the restrictive terms of the Edict of Nantes. The importance of sustaining his resolution to enforce the letter of the law cannot be over-stated, for the edict met with widespread disapproval and resistance from many quarters [*Docs* 4 and 5]. To begin with, it would need to be registered in the various parlements, which were judicial courts whose role was to register and to enforce the law. The most important of these was the parlement of Paris whose jurisdiction covered about two thirds of France and was considered to be the superior of the provincial parlements. Unhappy with the confessional compromise contained in the edict, the Paris parlement refused to register it for ten months until the king finally exercised his right to hold a *lit de justice*, that is to attend a session of parlement in person and to force its registration. In doing so, he was delivering a strong message. While he was willing to be accommodating and patient, as king he expected, ultimately, to be obeyed. The edict was finally registered, and the king's will prevailed. Yet it should not be overlooked that the parlement introduced some alterations, further reducing the permitted sites of worship for the Huguenots. Thus, there were clearly limits to the king's ability to impose the settlement, and the opposition to it was entrenched, active and effective.

As with previous edicts of pacification, to be successful the Edict of Nantes could not simply be pronounced and then registered. It had to be enforced and, indeed, interpreted for the particular circumstances that applied in countless localities throughout France. To this end, royal commissioners were named to each region. There they encountered simmering confessional tensions and were faced with many petitions and intractable legal conflicts which involved them ever more closely in municipal politics. Their success required a combination of determination and authority but also flexibility or sensitivity to local concerns and conditions. In sum, this peace was not the result of theological insight or enlightened dedication to modern notions of toleration. It was a difficult and imperfect effort to reinforce the king's traditional legal right to make law. Its success, however, is demonstrated by the fact that both Catholics and Protestants tended, henceforth, to appeal to royal justice to redress their grievances, not to a call to arms.

THE RECOVERY OF ROYAL AUTHORITY

Just as important as finding a military and confessional settlement for the stability of the new Bourbon dynasty was restoring the traditional fidelity of the nobility to the crown. Having only recently emerged from civil war, in which many of France's leading nobles had fought in opposition to Henri IV's succession to the throne, this would require a good deal of diplomacy in addition to many appeals to the nobles' innate sense of duty to their prince. On the whole, the king chose to be generous with his erstwhile enemies, offering full pardons, and often lucrative pensions, in exchange for formal declarations of obedience. While this strategy succeeded in pacifying the majority, the danger of armed, noble rebellion did not disappear altogether, and at times Henri IV also had to act quite forcefully. In 1602, for example, he faced a rebellion led by the Duke of Biron who was arrested, tried for treason and executed. Most of the other nobles implicated pleaded for forgiveness, though one, the Duke of Bouillon, who had aspired to the Huguenot leadership after Henri IV's conversion, went on to lead another revolt a few years later. The latter was put down by an army led by the king himself [*Doc.* 6]. Although neither rebellion posed a very serious challenge, they had been led by men who had previously received royal favour, revealing the fragility of the peace the king had established with his most powerful subjects. Recreating a stable, mutually-profitable relationship with the nobility would remain an elusive goal of the French crown for many decades.

Henri IV was particularly uneasy with the highest ranking nobles, the princes of the blood, for they posed the greatest threat to his dynastic ambitions. Although the king had managed to establish his own legitimacy, there were lingering doubts about the validity of his divorce from his first wife and, therefore, to the succession of his children by Marie de Medici whom he married in 1600. Henri II, Prince of Condé, for one, was a Bourbon prince himself. He had been heir presumptive prior to the birth of Louis XIII and, therefore, retained a plausible future claim to the throne and was always considered a potentially serious focus of future rebellion. In 1609, possibly partly due to inappropriate advances by Henri IV to his bride, Condé went into exile, from where the threat of revolt in alliance with foreign powers consequently grew.

Henri IV faced pressure from another quarter too. Some of his loyal followers felt aggrieved and excluded by the extension of royal favour to his former enemies and wished to be included on the royal council. The Count of Soissons, another of Henri IV's relations, also had a claim to the throne and was another potential focus of rebellion. For this reason he, too, was excluded from the royal council, specifically in favour of Sully. This was all part of an emerging trend of excluding the higher nobility from the council. In his difficult dealings with his nobles, Henri IV tried to resist their demands in order to name only loyal appointees. In this way, the council could act as direct representatives of the royal will. No longer could the most powerful noblemen simply assume a place or expect, in this way, to monopolise the king's ear and direct royal policy. Thus, just as the council was to be the instrument for the enforcement of the religious settlement, it was also to act, and be seen to be acting, as a neutral arbiter in all manner of legal disputes. The widespread acceptance of this role of the royal council was an important legacy of Henri IV's reign, something that Richard Bonney has identified as a distinctly 'Bourbon style of government' (Bonney, 1989).

Although Sully was a noble of considerable lineage and stature, this is not what earned him his favour. He was included on the council solely because he was a loyal and able servant of the king. His career is by far the most significant of the royal councillors, for indeed he, more than anybody else, embodied the administrative style of Henri IV's reign. Named Superintendent of Finance in 1598, Sully went on to acquire other responsibilities, including the grand-mastership of the artillery, and eventually established his pre-eminence on the royal council. In particular, Sully kept a firm grip on the royal treasury. Indeed, from 1605, all of the crown's important financial documents carried his signature only. Thus it was that he became the first of a series of minister-favourites in the seventeenth century who would dominate the royal council and who would be largely responsible for the daily administration of the country. This, as much as anything else, characterised the government of the Bourbon monarchs until 1661.

Sully's more immediately obvious legacy included improvements to the network of roads and the construction of canals and bridges, along with a number of architectural achievements in Paris and elsewhere. Yet he is also credited with the highly unusual situation in which the crown found itself in 1610 of actually enjoying a healthy budget surplus. Sully undoubtedly deserves his reputation for administrative competence. He kept a tight control on royal expenditure while trying to increase revenues. This he did by trying to root out corruption and inefficiency in the tax collection system, especially that of what was essentially a hearth tax, the *taille*, the main direct tax. A number of *chambres de justice* were held, which were formal investigations into the affairs of a given tax official or collector, which could lead to fines, arrest, imprisonment, or worse. He also increased other indirect taxes, the most important of which was the *gabelle*, a tax on salt. *Élus*, or tax collection officers who were directly responsible to the Paris government, were introduced in certain provinces. This was not the extent of his attempts at change, however. At times, he even tried to restrict the power of the courts, such as the chamber of accounts. As a theoretically 'sovereign court' of the realm, it objected to Sully's rather forceful and direct methods of administration.

One must be careful, however, not to exaggerate Sully's accomplishments. His success was achieved largely by debt restructuring. In other words, only by refusing to honour many of the debts that had accumulated during the civil wars was he able to put the royal finances on a sound footing. That he was able to do this without ruining the king's credit rating is probably a more important achievement than the budget surplus itself, which dissipated very quickly and to no great effect after he left office in 1611. Similarly, one must be careful not to read into Sully's actions a careful, deliberate plea to centralise government or to increase the crown's tax-raising powers for their own sake. His primary aim was simply to raise as much money as possible, and for this reason there are seemingly contradictory elements to his administration. Often taxes were simply farmed out. That is to say that speculators were allowed to bid for the right to collect a given tax for an area. From the crown's point of view, the competitive bidding could ensure a good price, and the cash was guaranteed by the tax farmer. For the financier involved, there was the possibility of collecting more than was invested. Also, the use of *élus*, which appears to have been an effort to over-ride provincial authorities and to increase the direct authority of the crown, was not systematic. Often their introduction was only threatened as a way of encouraging co-operation. Similarly, the *chambres de justice* were often invoked simply in the hope of extracting a financial 'gift' which could be exchanged for a pardon or for turning a blind eye to dubious practices. In other words, it seems that innovations were attempted for the immediate effect they would have on revenue, not on the longer-term ability of the state to exercise its authority.

Equally, Sully was not determined to make use of special commissioners or to oppose the existing administrative structure, even when it proved inefficient or reluctant to co-operate. In other words, his efforts were intended, not to over-ride, but to massage and to coerce the existing system. The most efficient way of doing this was to fill it with his own clients, people who were personally loyal to him. This allowed for his near complete domination of the state's finances, and in the process Sully accumulated a considerable personal fortune. Naturally, this caused a great deal of resentment. His political enemies, and subsequent historians, have seen in his considerable wealth evidence of self-serving ambition, corruption and duplicity. As it happens, his wealth (much of which was invested in property) can be accounted for by his offices and various gifts from the king (Aristide, 1989). From Henri IV's perspective, Sully earned his rewards. If there was anything untoward about his methods, this was better left unmentioned. The richer Sully became, the more influence he had, and the better he could manipulate the system to the king's advantage. This blurring of public and private finances was to their mutual benefit.

On balance, therefore, the reign of Henri IV was remarkably successful, and out of the peculiar circumstances of his accession to power patterns emerged which allow us to define a particular style of government. This was based upon an emphasis on the personal authority of the king within his council. He was also largely successful at insisting upon his traditional monopoly over the exercise of justice within the kingdom. The religious settlement of the Edict of Nantes, as the most obvious example, had not been an appeal to toleration or mutual understanding, nor was it an especially inspired blueprint for peaceful co-existence. It was, instead, a legal compromise and a statement of the royal will that would require a forceful implementation by the crown. In most cases, people longed for stability by 1598 and, therefore, tolerated the lead taken by the royal council in this respect. The main foreign threat had been, and would remain, Spanish Habsburg power. Accordingly, Henri IV celebrated his role as a warrior-king, ready to defend the interests of the kingdom. Just before he died, he had proved himself again to be willing and able, by preparing for a military intervention in nearby Cleves-Julich to thwart Habsburg designs to influence the succession to the local ruling bishop. Finally, the factional divisions that had so weakened previous reigns could be avoided in the future only if the royal council were to be seen as a neutral expression of the king's authority, not dominated by noble influence. This created a situation whereby the routine administration was to be conducted by personal favourites and increasingly by a single principal minister who, for practical reasons, would need to exercise considerable personal financial and political influence to keep the wheels of government turning.

THE EARLY REIGN OF LOUIS XIII

On 14 May 1610, Henri IV was attacked and killed in his carriage on the way to a military inspection in Paris by a lone, Catholic fanatic. The assassin's blade not only cut short the king's life, but it struck at the very heart of the monarchy itself by revealing the fragility of his achievements. His son immediately took the throne as Louis XIII, but at only eight years of age, government would be conducted by a regent, the Italian princess Marie de Medici, as Queen Mother. As in the past during a royal minority, the crown was now prone to the dangers of political in-fighting at court, and latent noble disaffection soon turned into outright rebellion. In 1614, Condé returned from exile to take up arms against the government. What made this particularly worrying is that this rebellion also enjoyed some limited support from the Huguenots, whose militancy remained a threat, awakening fears of a return to a state of endemic civil war [*Doc. 8*].

Partly for this reason, the regency government of Marie de Medici has not always been favourably treated by historians in contrast to the age of Henri IV. In some ways, it seems that the Queen Mother undid the work of the previous reign. By forcing Sully out of office in 1611, for instance, she lost a valuable servant and aroused concerns among the Huguenots that their fragile rights would soon be eroded or worse, thereby exacerbating the fears of the militants among their number. The budget surplus she inherited was soon gone in an effort to 'buy off' threatening nobles, and the best she can be credited with by some is survival. Yet under the circumstances, survival should not be under-rated as an achievement. In a manner reminiscent of her dead husband's approach, Marie de Medici took immediate steps to shore up her fledgling regency against the three principal threats to the monarchy: confessional, foreign, and political. She tried to reassure both sides of the confessional divide of her intentions with regard to the religious settlement by formally re-confirming the terms of the Edict of Nantes. Similarly, the potentially dangerous Cleves-Julich campaign was called off, and instead she arranged a double marriage, one between her son, Louis XIII, and the Spanish princess, Anne of Austria, and the other between her daughter and the future king of Spain. Such marriages were a traditional way of cementing international alliances, giving them solemnity and permanence, in part because they involved vows taken before God, in a way in which mere negotiated agreements could not. Most of all, they bound families, crucial in an age when it was hard to distinguish between states, as we understand them today, and ruling dynasties. Finally, in addition to simply trying to placate troublesome elements of the nobility with rewards and honours, Marie de Medici demonstrated a commitment to continuity with Henri IV's reign by leaving the conduct of government largely in the hands of the former administration, specifically those of the experienced ministers Villeroy, Sillery and Jeannin. Only the removal of Sully from office might appear to have been short-sighted. Yet, at the very least, this was consistent with the tendency of the previous reign to keep the upper nobility from the council. After all, Sully's value and his effectiveness as an administrator had been based upon his personal loyalty to Henri IV, and as such he would be less useful to the Queen Mother.

Despite addressing the principal threats to the crown in this way, the regency government suffered from widespread resentment of what was perceived to be an inept, equivocal, foreign queen. More specifically, and more dangerously, elements of the upper nobility were outraged at being kept from having any real influence at court. Although Condé's rebellion of 1614 was put down relatively easily, the grievances that had led to armed resistance were not addressed. Increasingly, Marie de Medici felt the pressure to summon an Estates-General, a rare meeting of leading representatives of the three 'estates' of French society: the clergy, the nobility and the commoners who were vaguely defined as the 'third estate'. This provided the opportunity for people to discuss and to compile a list of grievances to be presented to the Queen Mother. Although the Estates-General had great symbolic significance as an embodiment of the French nation, it was a consultative body only with no executive or legislative power, and it was convened and disbanded at the pleasure of the crown. There would be demands for other such meetings in the 1640s and 1650s, but the Estates-General that Marie de Medici called in 1614 would be the last for nearly two centuries. The government promised to consider carefully the concerns expressed, though it does not appear that there was any real intention to do much about them. Moreover, the selection of delegates had been so carefully managed that individuals like Condé had had no opportunity to gather political support for their personal ambitions (Hayden, 1974).

From the government's perspective, valuable time had been won by the Estates-General, and for this reason it looked as if it had weathered the storm. That year, Louis XIII reached the age of majority which promised to bring with it some stability. With the king now ruling in his own name, rebellion could no longer be justified on the grounds that it was directed, not against the person of the king, but merely against his 'wicked' advisors. Henceforth, it would be hard to interpret rebellion as anything but treason. By this time too, the government was being led by the ambitious Carlo Concini, Marshal Ancre. He had used the influence that his wife had with the Queen Mother to advance his own political career and consolidate his position at court. Eventually, Concini had the older ministers dismissed and replaced by a younger group of the Queen Mother's favourites.

For Louis XIII, there were two problems with Concini. First, his influence at court antagonised many nobles. In 1616, the troublesome Condé was arrested on Concini's orders, sparking another noble rebellion. Second, Louis XIII would not be able to overlook the fact that Concini was a political client and servant of the Queen Mother. Arguably, as power had increasingly concentrated in Concini's hands, government reflected more directly the wishes of Marie de Medici and had thus become more efficient. Nevertheless, having reached his majority, the king would need to be seen to be in charge himself. Whatever advantages or strengths Concini brought to government, from Louis XIII's perspective henceforth his influence could be only divisive and disruptive. If the government were to continue to attempt to impose stability during the king's majority, it could not be seen as the factional triumph of the Queen Mother's favourite and his clients. Specifically, if there was to be a favoured political figure at court, he would have to be a neutral servant of the king himself.

Encouraged by a confidant, Charles d'Albert, later the Duke of Luynes, Louis XIII attempted to consolidate his authority and to seize the reins of power by arranging for the assassination of Concini in April 1617 and sending his mother into exile at the palace of Blois. This unusual political murder can be seen as a jealous and petulant act by an awkward, impressionable adolescent. In other ways, however, it can be seen as a valiant attempt to protect and to build on the work of Henri IV. By taking the initiative and insisting on his own place at the centre of government, and more immediately by reinstating the former ministers who had served his father, Louis XIII was probably hoping to appeal to those who looked back fondly to the previous reign. To be sure, the wisdom of this move was not immediately obvious. Luynes quickly became a figure of hatred himself, resented both for the new-found wealth and for the monopoly of influence over the king that minister-favourites enjoyed. Moreover, in the exiled Queen Mother, the malcontents had a figure behind whom to rally, and thus they represented a serious, renewed military threat. In 1620, however, two determined efforts by Louis XIII went a long way to establishing his personal authority and, significantly, his willingness and ability to enforce it. These were the defeat in August of rebel forces fighting in the name of Marie de Medici at the Ponts-de-Cé, just south of the Loire, and by the reunion of Béarn to the kingdom of France soon thereafter.

Béarn was a Protestant province on the mountainous border with Spain that was also part of the independent kingdom of Navarre that had straddled the Pyrenees. The crowns of Navarre and France had been brought together when Henri IV became king of France. Yet the province had been excluded from the terms of the Edict of Nantes which meant that the Catholic minority there had no legal protection at all. This was a problem for Louis XIII. He had been raised a devout Catholic, and the situation in Béarn was an unacceptable compromise with 'heretics' and a stain on the reputation of the monarchy. In the summer of 1620, he led an army south to enforce the legal incorporation of Béarn into France and to re-establish Catholicism there. Militarily, the campaign was a huge success. After the long march south, Béarn capitulated to the royal army without a struggle, recognising that its long-term interests would not be best served by resisting the royal will. This had been a bold, potentially dangerous move, yet Louis XIII was at pains to stress that he had not simply seized an opportunity to flex his military muscles but rather to enforce his rightful legal and spiritual authority. Technically, the union of Béarn was not illegal, which was an important condition for the king, and there was no subsequent attempt constitutionally to dissolve it, or Navarre, into a greater unified France. Many of the province's legal traditions were respected, along with its identity, as reflected in the fact that henceforth the Bourbon kings of France always styled themselves 'kings of France and of Navarre', and both realms were represented in the king's arms (Desplat, 1991).

This sensitivity to legal niceties and Louis XIII's relatively limited ambitions at Béarn were typical of French kings. The crown had managed to maintain its authority during the difficult Wars of Religion largely through a legal process put in place to enforce a contested series of edicts of pacification (Roberts, 2004). For Louis XIII, there was a similar equation between the enforcement of the specific terms of his father's religious settlement and his own authority as king. Despite clearly harbouring a desire to rule a uniformly Catholic realm, he enforced with great passion the letter of the law and never attempted to exceed it at the expense of the Huguenots. By restoring Catholic worship in Béarn in 1620, through the strict application of the terms of the Edict of Nantes, Louis XIII had not only begun to build a military reputation of his own but continued the long process of consolidation of the interdependent legal and religious pillars of monarchical power. For the rest of the reign, legal justice continued to play a defining role for Louis XIII who particularly cherished his reputation as 'Louis the Just' (Moote, 1989).

This was an important year also because Louis XIII was anxious to enforce the obedience that traditionally bound his nobility, and with the victory at the Ponts-de-Cé he successfully brought the current spate of noble rebellions to an end. Despite his successes of 1620, however, the monarchy's challenges had not been met entirely. The union of Béarn awoke deep-seated fears among the Huguenots elsewhere in France. In December 1620, an assembly of the Huguenot, or 'Reformed' church, as it was known, met at the western sea port of La Rochelle, their most significant remaining centre of strength, in order to organise their armed resistance to any more such campaigns by the crown. This was strictly forbidden under the terms of the Edict of Nantes and was, therefore, immediately declared illegal by Louis XIII and ordered to disband. Looking back, we know that nearly another decade of the already long history of religious, civil war was re-opening. This brought with it the threat of renewed foreign intervention in France, just as the recent outbreak in 1618 of what would become known as the Thirty Years' War in the German empire threatened international peace. Moreover, the fact that Louis XIII was still fighting to force the acquiescence of an awkward nobility, best personified by Condé, suggests that the stability and social order craved by his father was to be an on-going project, not just the fruit of these two campaigns in 1620.

PART TWO   ANALYSIS

CHAPTER TWO

RELIGION

French kings derived their authority from God. They were divinely appointed and were even considered to have some limited, sacred powers. This was most strikingly demonstrated in occasional ceremonies during which the king's 'royal touch' was believed to cure a severe skin condition, known as scrofula. Yet kings were not, themselves, divine. They were the human representatives of God's authority, acting as the guardians, or stewards, of the kingdom. Thus France was not the personal property of kings to do with as they pleased. Indeed, just as their legitimacy depended upon God, so they were beholden to Him and had inherited limits to their authority, along with certain responsibilities. These conditions were spelled out in the coronation oath. Kings were required to respect and to protect the interests of their subjects. Although this logic was not extended to allow resistance to kings who abused their authority, they were still subject to divine law. This was a restriction which kings rarely, if ever, wilfully disregarded. To be accused of tyranny, in particular, was anathema, for it implied a breach of responsibilities and the inevitable collapse of legitimacy. Specifically, kings were to defend the French church and to root out and eradicate heresy. The political fighting and civil wars that occurred because of Henri IV's succession threatened to weaken the authority of the crown in the sixteenth century. Yet both sides of the confessional divide had been keen to protect the sacred nature of the monarchy. Indeed, it was precisely because the religious sensibilities of both sides had been challenged that people took up arms. Many Catholics were determined to defend the purity of the monarchy from the 'stain' of heresy; Henri IV's supporters, on the other hand, saw themselves as members of the 'true' church, and they insisted that the divinely-ordained succession must be respected. In the seventeenth century, then, religion continued not simply to justify the authority of the reign but to shape its progress. When, for example, Louis XIII led his army to re-impose Catholic worship in Béarn in 1620 and began threatening the Huguenots elsewhere, he was not simply shoring up his military authority for its own sake but performing his sacred duty, as he saw it.

THE CATHOLIC REFORMATION

Louis XIII's treatment of the Huguenots in the decade after 1620 was heavy-handed, to say the least, an indication that enforcing his religious authority, and the justice of the religious settlement in particular, remained a top priority. His earnestness reflects much more than just his personal inclinations, however, for it was entirely consistent with the renewed religious fervour, and often militant Catholicism, both within and without government, which characterised the first half of the seventeenth century. Across Europe, the Catholic church had long been in the process of reform and rejuvenation. It had undergone a thorough reassessment of its practices and teachings and had determined to take a more direct role in the lives of its parishioners. This process found its definitive expression in the decrees of the Council of Trent, which met inter-mittently between 1543 and 1563 and which sought to eradicate superstition and to invigorate and unify religious practices at the parish level. This was to be done through greater clerical training and discipline, enforced through routine visitations by bishops. As a useful label, it is still referred to as the 'Counter Reformation', that is to say a response to the Protestant challenge of the sixteenth century, though many historians prefer simply to refer to a 'Catholic Reformation', for the church had its own independent, internal traditions of reform. Either way, Catholic reform deeply affected seventeenth-century French society.

The demands of the Council of Trent (or the 'Tridentine' decrees) were problematic, however. Within the French church, there was a long-established spirit of relative independence from Rome, or Gallicanism, which made Tridentine reform with its implication of papal supremacy difficult to endorse formally. Several powerful institutions, such as the parlement of Paris, along with the theological faculty of the University of Paris (the Sorbonne), and indeed a large part of the clergy in France, were opposed. Moreover, for Henri IV, as a king whose authority largely rested on the precarious Edict of Nantes and its limited toleration of Protestant 'heresy', it would have been impossible to accept legally the unyielding terms of the Council of Trent. Yet it was the association with the papacy specifically that made the Tridentine reforms especially unpalatable to many people. The principle of reform or renewal of the French church itself was actually widely endorsed.

A clear indication of a widespread, renewed spiritual enthusiasm in the early seventeenth century is the increased number of lay societies, or confraternities. These groups, sanctioned by the church, or affiliated with a specific religious order, provided mutual support for lay people and regularly met for prayers or to hear mass. They often did charitable work, conducted public processions and so forth. More obviously, since the late sixteenth century, the monastic orders had also experienced an explosion in numbers and a renewed commitment to piety. The Society of Jesus (that is to say, the

Jesuits) is a good example. Though it originated in Spain and already had its first house in France by 1540, it represents for many historians the quintessence of the Counter Reformation with its emphasis on education and missionary work. Resented by many Gallicans for their devotion to the papacy, and at times even banned from France on these grounds, the Jesuits were nevertheless enormously influential following their reinstatement in the country by Henri IV in 1603 after a brief hiatus. They provided confessors to the Bourbon kings and education to many of the children of the French nobility [*Doc. 22*].

Other religious orders and seminaries were also founded, introduced from abroad or simply re-invigorated, either through stricter observance of monastic vows and greater discipline or by the foundation of new sub-groups. The Capuchins, for example, an austere branch of the Franciscans introduced to France in 1575, were known for their commitment to preaching. In 1618, a group of reformed Benedictine monks, the Maurists, was established to renew the commitment to the austerity of St Benedict and, in this case, also to historical scholarship and to the preservation of religious works. Certain individuals, too, personify the dual commitment to both Catholic orthodoxy or spiritual discipline and to the invigoration of a strong church, visible and active within the community. In François de Sales and Vincent de Paul, for example, who founded religious houses and whose own high-profile charitable and educational work led to their eventual canonisation, we see clear evidence of officially endorsed, and genuine, efforts towards the spiritual re-invigoration of France. Along with Pierre de Bérulle, who founded the Oratory, a group dedicated to training and supporting priests, these were among the most influential reformers of the early seventeenth century, perfectly embodying the spirit of the Counter Reformation in France.

Politically, the more active, proscriptive, and intrusive spirit of reform appealed to a monarch who wished to impose his spiritual authority. This less edifying, authoritarian aspect of the Counter Reformation church is most evident with respect to the treatment of women. In the first half of the seventeenth century, at least twenty-four religious houses for men were founded in Paris alone, but twice that number for women. It is possible to see these houses as partly punitive, corrective institutions for unwilling women, representing a sharp rise of strict paternal authority, or even misogyny, in the French church (Rapley, 1990). Indeed, recent work has stressed the tendency of the Counter Reformation, in general, to suppress women's ambitions. Yet such a perspective fails to account entirely for the startling growth of convents. Certainly, the new orders also had laudable ambitions. Many were devoted to quiet prayer and contemplation, such as the Carmelites (introduced to France in 1604). Increasingly, more orders for women were devoted to teaching, such as the Ursulines, established in France in 1592, or to charitable work in the community, such as the Daughters of Charity, founded in 1633. Furthermore, as Barbara Diefendorf has recently illustrated, in practice these new foundations actually offered women genuine opportunities for spiritual growth and an active role in the life of the church. By bringing to light the more direct influence on the character of these houses of local lay patrons (and their money) than that of the church hierarchy or indeed of the state, Diefendorf's work also serves as a caution against assuming that a resurgent Catholic church was simply a tool of a monarchy intent on increasing its authority rather than a reflection of genuine spiritual renewal (Diefendorf, 2001).

Some historians have emphasised the limits of the effectiveness of the Catholic Reformation, especially in affecting the spiritual lives of people in the countryside. Yet the seventeenth century still deservedly upholds its reputation for spiritual revival and energy. Though the increase in the number of confraternities and other religious foundations began to tail off by mid-century, all of this activity had had a remarkable impact on French society. Even the architectural landscape of the principal cities of France was affected, with hundreds of colleges and chapels built. This construction, often in flamboyant baroque style, was more than matched by the visual impact made by the unparalleled productivity of royal architects commissioned with projects like the completion of the *pont neuf* in Paris in 1598, the first open bridge across the Seine, and by such civic projects as the construction of the imposing *hôtel de ville*, or city hall, of Paris which began in earnest in 1605. France's *grand siècle* is clearly reflected in the architectural outpouring of the seventeenth century which still adorns Paris, in particular, with many of its most familiar landmarks.

Many overtly political and personal projects were undertaken such as the Luxembourg Palace by Marie de Medici. Of course, the massive expansion of the Louvre and the palace of the Tuileries alone attest to the determination of the crown to leave its physical mark too. Such work went hand in hand with a wider trend for the nobility, in general, to build grand hotels, or personal urban residences. Of particular note in the context of spiritual renewal, however, is the Val-de-Grâce church that was built by Anne of Austria. In 1621, she founded a convent for Benedictine nuns in a Paris suburb which she often visited for worship and as a retreat from the pressures of court life. Anne's personal problems stemmed not just from being away from her native Spain but from her failure to provide an heir to her husband. When she finally gave birth in 1638 to the future Louis XIV, it came as if by miracle. She determined then to erect a church on the site as an act of thanksgiving. In 1645, the young Louis XIV himself laid the cornerstone of the grand, new baroque chapel and expanded convent, perfectly embodying the inextricable bond between religion and political power in the architectural iconography of the Catholic Reformation. Taken together, all of this building provided a profound and lasting visual statement of the resurgent strength of both the French church and the royal state.

There was a tangible increase in the church's profile, therefore, but also in genuine religious enthusiasm and piety. Despite some well-founded reservations about the full impact of Catholic reform, on the whole it can be said that it resulted in a more efficient, dedicated church hierarchy and, among the population, in greater literacy and more intimate understanding of Catholic doctrine. Although it must be reiterated that this process was not driven by a self-consciously authoritarian monarchy, it did correspond closely with the spiritual and practical instincts of the crown. In a sense, the Counter Reformation was an age of confident revival in both religion and in government. The interdependence of the two, that is of church and state, was most eloquently expressed (less publicly, though no less profoundly for it) in 1638 in a ceremony staged by Louis XIII which formally placed the kingdom under the protection of the Virgin Mary. It is equally clear in his choice of political advisors.

THE CARDINAL MINISTERS

Cardinals Richelieu and Mazarin, who were the principal ministers for Louis XIII and Louis XIV from 1624–42 and 1643–61 respectively, are two of the most familiar names from French history. Richelieu, a reforming bishop from the relatively poor bishopric of Luçon, came into politics as a client of Marie de Medici which included a brief period on the royal council in 1616–17. After re-joining the council in 1624, he quickly earned the trust of Louis XIII and consolidated his grip on power. Cardinal Mazarin, Richelieu's hand-picked successor, led the government through the difficult years of the mid-century with the same presumption of unassailable political control that had characterised Richelieu's ministry. Though their reputations contrast somewhat, their approaches to government were broadly similar, and in some respects their claim to the reins of power and their monopoly on the king's ear define these years as a unique period of government. Of course, the whole period from the beginning of Sully's pre-eminence by 1605 to Mazarin's death in 1661 can properly be seen to be one of 'government by minister-favourite' (Elliott and Brockliss, 1999). Yet the stature of Richelieu and Mazarin, in particular, was unparalleled, and their roles as cardinals of the Catholic church, which until very recently have not received the attention they deserve from historians, also set their period of government apart.

Traditionally, Richelieu's career has been viewed very positively. In large part, he was the author of his own reputation, with historians broadly accepting his assessment of his career as revealed in his memoirs and particularly in his *testament politique* [Doc. 24]. In this, he claimed to have come to the royal council with a clear, three-part plan for the reform of the kingdom. Appealing directly to the three most deeply held concerns of the king, for whom it was ostensibly written, he said he aimed to root out heresy and destroy the Huguenots, to check the power of the Spanish Habsburgs abroad, and to tame the pride of the nobility. All of this, he also claims to have achieved. Mazarin, on the other hand, suffered from the damaging effects of the internal upheavals and violent conflicts of the Fronde, for which many of his contemporaries, and subsequent historians, have blamed him. Sandwiched between the imposing edifice of Richelieu's ministry and the glory of the personal rule of Louis XIV, Mazarin has been much less revered and is often associated with the financial chaos, war-weariness and widespread rebellion which plagued his time in office. Their contrasting reputations, however, should not disguise the coherence of the period of the two ministries. Both careers were inextricably linked to, and shaped by, the war with Spain from 1635 to 1659, and their political style largely grew out of the enormous financial and administrative pressures that arose from it. Much work has been done on the nature of their political careers, though Richelieu has been the more popular subject of study. As a result of this work, we can no longer see Richelieu (even less Mazarin) as politically omnipotent, able simply to impose their will. The pressures of conducting the war and domestic political dangers did not even allow the luxury of seriously entertaining grand schemes to modernise the French state. Their careers were far more pragmatic than once thought, driven by the day-to-day concerns of government rather than by political ideals or ideological purpose.

Richelieu and Mazarin also share reputations as cynical, political manipulators who simply used religion for their own ends. It is clear, especially from detailed work by Joseph Bergin, that the church was an important institution not only for advancing family interests through appointments to key positions but also for exerting wider political influence (Bergin, 1992). Immediately upon re-joining the royal council in 1624, Richelieu successfully argued that his position as a cardinal (which he had attained in 1622) should give him a natural political pre-eminence. It is no co-incidence, then, that Mazarin, who had come to Richelieu's attention as a papal envoy in the 1630s, also became a cardinal and relied on this ecclesiastical standing to justify his political authority. However, in contrast to Richelieu's early career which saw him rise rapidly through the church hierarchy, Mazarin had never been ordained a priest. While on one hand this might suggest that the cardinalate had become nothing more than a political tool cynically exploited, on the other, the fact that a high rank within the Catholic Church could provide political legitimacy could simply be seen as a further indication of the interdependence of political authority and the vibrant Catholic church in France.

Although Richelieu used his position in the church to advance his own interests and as a tool of the government, this is not inconsistent with sincere religious belief or passion for Catholic reform. He wrote a number of works on theological subjects, and his early career as a bishop along with his subsequent behaviour as a cardinal reveals nothing to suggest that his faith was anything but genuine or that his interest in the welfare of the church was not real. In the nomination of new bishops, we see most clearly the combination of political and spiritual motives at work. In theory, at least, one of the most remarkable features of the French monarchy was the king's right to name bishops to vacant sees, a right negotiated from the pope by the Concordat of Bologna of 1516, which gave him enormous potential patronage power. Defending this control over the nomination of bishops was essential to the crown's influence over the church and to any effort to improve the spiritual health of the realm, for often in practice when a position became available there was enormous political pressure from leading noble families to nominate one of their members or clients which the king often found hard to ignore, even if the candidate was under age. As Richelieu's political and ecclesiastical influence grew, he was able to affect decision making, not simply to choose men loyal to him and to the crown, but those who would support his reforming ambitions. Although political considerations in nominations did not disappear altogether, it seems that a genuine concern about the quality of the candidates and their willingness to take their position seriously had become an important criterion for selection. Thus, while Richelieu's personal and political interests informed some of the choices, it seems nevertheless that the overall quality of the episcopate also improved (Bergin, 1999).

The demands of government were not always so easily wedded to reforming religious zeal, however. Richelieu's career was hampered by the political opposition of a faction at court referred to as the *dévots*, who wanted the interests of the Catholic church put ahead of any national or secular concerns. Although originally a *dévot* himself, in that he shared the same vision for the church, conflict quickly arose primarily over Richelieu's diplomatic priority of containing the power of Catholic Spain, even if it meant allying with Protestant powers abroad or failing to root out the last vestiges of Protestantism within France. Prior to the formal declaration of war by France against Spain in 1635, the government supported Protestant princes in Germany and, most notably, the campaigns of the Swedish King Gustavus Adolphus. For most historians, and for many of those at court, this was a sign of Richelieu's lack of spiritual integrity and, worse, of his naked political ambition.

Much of Richelieu's attention was taken up by this foreign policy and by the war, yet it does not seem that he was the aggressive, French nationalist that has often been portrayed. His policies were not designed to push France to some imaginary 'natural boundaries' as was once commonly assumed. Rather, his concern was with maintaining bridgeheads across the Rhine or the Alps in order to be able to maintain French influence abroad and to keep the Habsburgs from consolidating their apparent universalist ambitions. As one historian has put it, his outlook was 'international' rather than national and 'Christian, rather than secular'. In other words, he saw his ultimate goal as the establishment of a lasting peace in Christendom, 'une bonne paix', guaranteed by the 'Most Christian' king of France (as French kings were officially styled), in which no one power, like Spain, could use the Catholic church as a vehicle for pursuing political domination of the continent [*Doc.* 17]. In the current circumstances, allying with Protestant powers was the only way to counter the Habsburg threat and to attempt to establish this lasting balance (Weber, 1992).

Though many people today might remain sceptical about the purity of Richelieu's motives abroad, it is clear that they did not arise from mere national, diplomatic interests alone but were also bound, to some extent at least, by the notion of the sacred duty of the king to protect the interests of the church. Working behind the scenes and informing many of Richelieu's policies was the Capuchin, Père Joseph, sometimes referred to as the *éminence grise*, whose crusading zeal and dedication to his patron made him an invaluable counsellor until his death in 1638. In the practical art of war, too, Richelieu saw no contradiction between an ecclesiastical and a military vocation [*Doc.* 21]. Indeed, typically, the military command at the time included such high-profile churchmen as the Cardinal of La Valette in the army and Henri d'Escoubleau de Sourdis, Archbishop of Bordeaux, in the navy, with no hint of a conflict of interests.

Religion imbued all aspects of the ministries of Richelieu and Mazarin. The reconstruction of the Sorbonne and particularly the chapel which Richelieu commissioned, is an eloquent expression of his recognition of the inter-connection of religious devotion, the arts and political power. Yet he was also interested in the many broader cultural developments of this age of Counter Reformation. Literature and art, as well as architecture, all flourished and all attracted the attention and patronage of the crown. Philippe de Champaigne, for example, was the court painter, responsible for providing many of the inspirational images that decorated the palaces of Paris, including Richelieu's own, the present-day Palais Royale, which was built across the street from the Louvre as an enduring symbol of his power and his closeness to the crown. Champaigne also painted many portraits at court and is responsible for many of the familiar images of Richelieu that we recognise today. In the *palais mazarin*, where the manuscript collection of the French National Library is housed today, we can see Mazarin's own taste in self-promoting display which was arguably even more flamboyant than Richelieu's. As well as being protector of the Royal Academy of Painting in 1648, Mazarin also commissioned many Italian painters.

In 1635, Richelieu founded the *académie française*, thereby guaranteeing in the minds of observers to the present day a direct, personal association with the development of the French language and literature. For some critics, offering his protection to what was effectively at the time a literary society, and other examples of state involvement in the arts, were simply ways of maintaining official control over the burgeoning, increasingly secular and potentially subversive literary and artistic circles of the day. While it is true that certain restrictions were placed on artistic freedom of expression, it is equally true that the monarchy, and Richelieu in particular, were eager to embrace and to encourage the cultural achievements of the reign. Rather than being motivated by the desire to control or to censor art, Richelieu hoped to indulge in, support, and to use it to his own ends as a celebration of his own power and of the glory of the realm. He had an ornate, new palace and extensive gardens built at his family's traditional home of Richelieu, in Poitou, for example, as a personal monument, reflecting and thereby reinforcing his authority. In 1635, he commissioned the influential painter, Nicolas Poussin (whose work was quite modern by being somewhat more secular than normal, often depicting scenes from antiquity) to provide paintings, including the 'Triumph of Neptune', to hang in a room dedicated to the celebration of Richelieu's personal authority over the French navy as Grand-Master of Navigation. Thus there is no inconsistency in the fact that Sourdis, a personal favourite to whom Richelieu would later give the command of the navy in battle against Spain, was also entrusted by his patron with overseeing the project to build this palace.

The image that the cardinal was constructing at Richelieu was of more than just an indulgent celebration of his own grandeur and personal wealth. This was an architectural project with the aim of positively reinforcing his political power that included the whole town, which was completely rebuilt and remains to this day an excellent, unspoilt example of seventeenth-century urban planning. Walled, square, with perpendicular, straight streets and a long central boulevard, the new town of Richelieu reflected the emerging emphasis on rationality that would come to affect the arts and sciences so profoundly in the future. It included a baroque parish church, dedicated to Our Lady of the Assumption, where Vincent de Paul founded the Lazarists on one of his frequent visits. The whole project was a powerful statement of Richelieu's social status and political authority, but also evidence of the self-conscious appropriation to the same end of the Counter Reformation, its theology and its mission, and all of its associated, modern cultural developments.

To be sure, the state tried (often in vain) to control culture. Yet this had at least as much to do with the opportunity it presented as any potential threat it posed. The two were to be mutually supportive, flourishing together. Patronage of the arts undoubtedly helped the political ambitions of Richelieu who worked, throughout his ministerial career, to three different, but complementary ends: political, personal, and religious. Ultimately, he worked in the service of the king and in the interests of the monarchy. He did this not just for its own sake, but because he knew that his own privileged position in French politics depended upon the king's goodwill, something which could be withdrawn at any time. He also worked to advance his own interests, as a typical seventeenth-century nobleman. That is to say that Richelieu pursued the interests of his family, building its name, its fortune and its influence in government. What was true of Richelieu was equally true of Mazarin, and it is no contradiction to say that at the same time both worked for the good of Christendom, as they saw it. There is no reason to doubt that they felt that ensuring a strong French monarchy, supported by a powerful and widely respected and influential principal minister, was the best way to protect the Catholic church from the 'tyranny' of the Spanish crown, just as it was the surest way to ensure religious conformity within France and the reform of the church [*Doc.* 18].

THE HUGUENOTS

On 28 October 1628, Louis XIII and Richelieu finally entered the gates of La Rochelle after having directed a royal army for over a year in an agonising, brutal siege. For the inhabitants of this last remaining, major military strong-hold of the Huguenot community on the western seaboard of France, the suffering had been appalling. Though estimates vary, a pre-siege population of about 28,000 had been reduced, mostly through starvation, to as few as 6,000. At its peak, the royal army which encircled the city numbered some 20,000. Completing the isolation of the city, and acting as an imposing symbol of the determination of the crown to bring the Huguenots to obedience, was an enormous dike that was built, over four months, across the mouth of the harbour and supported by a number of new, purpose-built royal warships. These ships were the particular responsibility of Richelieu who also had overall command of military operations in the area in the king's absence. The dramatic scenes and the decisiveness of the victory have ensured that the siege has retained a place in the popular imagination. For historians, it has long stood as a watershed, concluding the seventeenth-century epilogue to the Wars of Religion by bringing to a final end any question of further Huguenot military resistance. At the same time, it is also seen as a first, major step in the consolidation of royal authority and the development of 'absolutism', a dominant theme in historical writing on the rest of the century. By associa-tion, this episode has also cemented Richelieu's reputation for determination, ruthlessness and dedication to the interests of the state.

It is a mistake, however, to suggest that the siege of La Rochelle was Richelieu's personal project. It was, on the contrary, the climax of a series of wars conducted by Louis XIII that had begun with the campaign to Béarn in 1620. For although the Huguenot community was far weaker than it had been in the sixteenth century, and one after another Huguenot towns opened their gates to the king's forces in the summer of 1621, militant elements remained within the community, and collectively the Huguenots still posed a serious political threat (James, 2002). Despite the many military successes in 1621 for Louis XIII, the campaigning season ended in failure when the royal army was forced to withdraw from the siege of the southern city of Montauban, the next most important Huguenot city after La Rochelle. Some historians simply blame the failure on the military incompetence of Luynes who died at the siege. Yet it seems that the crown faced greater dangers than this. By the time they had arrived before Montauban, winter was approaching and time was running out. In addition, in some areas, Huguenot resistance was actually quite fierce, and more ominously their attempts at a national military organisation had been surprisingly successful. At the same time that the Huguenots in the south were vigorously defending Montauban and forcing a royal retreat, along the west coast a Huguenot fleet, which operated out of La Rochelle in the name of the assembly of the Huguenot church, was proving superior to that of the crown itself.

Fortune turned decidedly towards the crown in April 1622, however, when royal forces, in their third successive year of campaigning, routed the Huguenots just to the north of La Rochelle. The rebels no longer seemed able to mount a successful resistance, and the Peace of Montpellier of October 1622 appeared to mark the final victory of the crown over both political and confessional rebellion against its authority. However, two more wars, in 1625–26 and 1627–29, would need to be fought before the crown could actually impose a final, military resolution to the long period of civil war in France, and it was clear that La Rochelle would have to be the primary target of the crown's energies. Significantly, in September 1625, improvised royal naval forces defeated a Huguenot fleet near La Rochelle. Yet the intervention of an English fleet under the Duke of Buckingham in 1627, sent in support of their co-religionists in France, once again raised the stakes. In July, Buckingham's troops occupied the strategic île de Ré, which lies just off La Rochelle. With this direct, foreign military intervention on French soil on behalf of the Huguenots, it was clear that a comprehensive solution was required. The English forces were eventually dislodged from the island in November. With their withdrawal, the full force of the crown's military energy could be directed at the ill fated city.

La Rochelle was peculiar in a number of ways. Not only was it a predominantly Huguenot city with formal ties to England, it had long enjoyed a tradition of virtual political independence from the French crown and a number of special fiscal liberties which it defended fiercely. One could, therefore, explain the crown's hostility in terms of its growing authority. There simply was no room in the France that was emerging in the seventeenth century, it is said, for such an anomaly. The city's very existence was a continuous affront to the crown's authority, and wresting control of the city, its port, and its overseas trade from the Huguenots was an understandable reaction and a clear expression by the government of what is often called 'mercantilist' intervention to direct the economy and to increase its control (Parker, 1983).

Yet there are no other, similar examples of such a dedicated effort to impose the crown's will by force at this time, which suggests that Louis XIII's pursuit of justice, in the specific form of the Edict of Nantes, rather than simply power for its own sake, is what motivated him. In many accounts, defeating the Huguenots decisively in the 1620s is presented as only a necessary first step before the more important problems of reforming the state or challenging the power of Spain abroad could be faced. Yet Louis XIII had options and need not have chosen the reduction of the city as his priority. Even Cardinal Richelieu, who is known in the popular imagination as the implacable enemy of the Huguenots and who famously remarked that 'there will never be peace in France as long as the Huguenots exist', initially advised shelving the Huguenot problem in order to deal with Spanish competition for influence in northern Italy. Louis XIII took the decision to defeat the Huguenots because religious conformity was a personal priority, born from his sense of duty as king to protect the integrity of the church and to eradicate 'heresy' from the realm that was entrusted to his care.

The terms of the Peace of Alès of 1629, which was eventually granted after some mopping up operations against continuing pockets of Huguenot resistance in the south, are often seen as curiously generous. Rather than outlawing Protestant worship altogether, Louis XIII chose simply to confirm the terms of the Edict of Nantes. After over sixty years of intermittent conflict, and after finally achieving decisive military victory, some asked why the crown should now choose to enforce a thirty-year-old compromise which grudgingly tolerated heretics. The answer is that it was precisely because the legitimacy of the crown had largely depended upon the enforcement of the edict and the legal and spiritual authority it embodied. It should be remembered that although the Edict of Nantes would still be enforced, the extra *brevets* and secret clauses which had allowed a certain, limited political and military protection would not be renewed. In other words, while in certain restricted situations freedom of Protestant worship would be permitted, as a political body capable of armed resistance the Huguenots were a spent force. In this sense, the king was not taking any substantial risks at all. More significantly, in this way, he could not be accused of having arbitrarily enforced his will against the established laws of his kingdom. Instead, despite taking up arms against his subjects, he was actually upholding the law and maintaining the distinction he had always held between 'loyal' and 'rebellious' Huguenots. By allowing Protestant worship for his loyal subjects, Louis 'the Just' was treating them fairly and justly. There is no question that his long-term ambition, as with his predecessors, was to rule a uniformly Catholic France. However, especially after the fall of La Rochelle, enforcing religious uniformity by force of arms would only bring diminishing returns and open the king to the damning charge of 'tyranny'.

After 1629, the Huguenots were no longer seen as a significant problem for the government, and under Richelieu and Mazarin they did not suffer any large-scale persecution. Yet despite a new spate of conversions and the long-term effects of assimilation, the number of Protestant worshippers in France and the strength of their community did not decline as rapidly as is often assumed (Benedict, 2001). By 1685, when the Edict of Nantes was famously revoked by Louis XIV, nearly one in twenty French people were still Huguenots. At a local level, where Huguenots lived in sufficient numbers, there was a relatively peaceful co-existence between the faiths, even a certain toleration. Politically, the Huguenots tried to protect themselves by professing their obedience to the crown. Most notably, during the Fronde, the Huguenots saw no advantage in taking up arms again. Instead, they maintained their loyalty to the government, seeing this as the surest way to safeguard their remaining privileges. In return, though they were never fully accepted by the crown, the Huguenots were largely left alone. The government did not feel pushed to take extreme military measures against them, though legally it continued to exert pressure and to erode their position. Despite the lingering presence of a Protestant minority in seventeenth-century France, therefore, this was far from a pluralist society. Seen in this light, the eventual revocation of the Edict of Nantes in 1685, though possibly ill-advised, was nevertheless not out of step with current thinking. On the contrary, it was the fulfilment of the long-held desire for a uniformly Catholic realm which was implicit in the terms of the Edict of Nantes and which befitted the legal and sacral nature of kings of France.

JANSENISM

The military resolution of the Huguenot 'problem' by 1629 did not spell the end of religious tensions and conflict. The crown's greatest difficulty henceforth came from disputes between reformers within the Catholic church. When a convent in Paris, the Port-Royal, broke from the Cistercian movement to form a new 'Order of the Holy Sacrament' following the teachings of a Flemish theologian, Cornelius Jansen, the movement that would come to be known as Jansenism began to attract attention in France. Heavily influenced by the writings of St Augustine, Jansen emphasised the role of God's grace in attaining salvation over that of human efforts. In this, some have identified a similarity with Calvinism. Yet Jansenists were loyal and devout Catholics, and their theology was most likely not the main cause of the animosity they attracted. The nuns of Port-Royal, and others who followed their theological lead as the movement flourished in the 1640s, were distrusted because their contemplative focus on the individual and their attraction to the simplicity of the early church fed a natural distrust of hierarchy, both of the church and of the state.

In 1638, the abbot of Saint-Cyran, who had publicly defended the Port-Royal nuns and influenced their teaching, was arrested on Richelieu's orders. To modern observers, this can seem an arbitrary exercise of political power.

Yet Richelieu's anxiety over Saint-Cyran is easily understood. The cardinal-minister would have found the Jansenists' regard for a Flemish authority, with its connection to the Spanish monarchy, unpalatable. On a personal political level, Saint-Cyran had ties to Richelieu's political foes, the *dévots*. Theologically, the Jansenists' teachings were dangerously close to heresy, but more than that their hostility to the state would have been an affront to the desire for a doctrinally unified Catholic Reformation under the direction of the king. Although the crown was clearly increasingly willing to use its power to direct people's religious lives, again one must be careful not to conclude from such interventions that it was being opportunistic and using religion simply as a way of controlling its subjects.

The persecution of the Jansenists might seem an over-reaction to the danger they actually posed, especially Louis XIV's decision in 1711 to raze Port-Royal to the ground having already brutally expelled the nuns and either imprisoned or sent into exile other leading Jansenists. Yet there were grounds for seeing them as potentially disruptive. By the 1640s, it was a growing movement that was running seminaries and attracting influential members, including intellectuals, bishops and leading members of the parlement. The movement was especially popular among the 'robe' nobility, that is those who served the crown, not with the military arts that traditionally conferred nobility, but in the administration and in the courts. It was just such groups who initially rebelled in the first, dangerous years of the Fronde from 1648. Jansenists also tended to lend their support to one of the most troublesome leaders of the subsequent civil uprisings, Jean-François Paul de Gondi, or the Cardinal de Retz as he was from 1653. Retz was particularly dangerous because he combined religious passion and authority with his political hatred of Mazarin. Though he spent a good deal of the 1650s in prison as a consequence, his influence was not so easily extinguished. As archbishop of Paris from 1653 (and coadjutor with his uncle prior to that), he had considerable local influence and enjoyed the support of most of the parish clergy.

Not only did Retz threaten the political loyalty of the capital in this way, but his anti-government protests went beyond expressing personal hatred of Mazarin or specific grievances about crown policy. The clergy who were bitter about Retz's arrest also resented government interference at the parish level. They wanted more independence and local influence, and in this way to some extent they challenged the spiritual authority of the crown. Although typical of most 'frondeurs' in that Retz did not want to see a revolutionary re-ordering of society or the abolition of the monarchy, merely its reform (along with greater power for himself), his popular support reveals a general reaction against the increasingly tight control of the church by the state, seen by many as too heavily influenced by the Jesuits (who were the great rivals of the Jansenists). Because of the many other serious political and military threats posed by the Fronde, it is easy to underestimate the significance of this religious element. Indeed Retz's political ambitions often seemed to outweigh any personal, religious convictions he might have held. Nevertheless, until long after the main struggle of the Fronde had been settled, criticism of the government still echoed from among the ranks of the Paris clergy, a phase of the troubles that has been called the 'religious Fronde' (Golden, 1981). It was not until Retz was forced to resign as archbishop and to repudiate Jansenism in 1661 that this period of civil disobedience came fully to an end. Whereas many of the other *frondeurs* subsequently received pardons from Louis XIV in his attempt to re-establish order, Retz did not. This suggests that the basis upon which he had opposed the crown was felt to have been particularly obnoxious.

Just as it is misleadingly easy to interpret the later revocation of the Edict of Nantes by Louis XIV as nothing but an ill-advised political decision arising from unbounded arrogance and insensitivity, so is it all too easy to be cynical about the strength of his personal religious conviction. Without doubt, he had an unquenchable thirst for power, and he celebrated this power in an elaborate, indulgent court life which (at least during his younger days) was far from a study of piety and self-restraint. Yet as with his predecessors, political power with all of its attendant trappings was not incompatible with sincere religious belief or a sense of duty. And Louis XIV certainly understood the central place the church held in the definition, and effective exercise, of his authority. It should be remembered that in 1654, in the immediate aftermath of the Fronde, when the upheaval was still very fresh in his mind, Louis XIV came of age and was crowned at the cathedral at Reims. Here, as dictated by tradition, the ceremony and the coronation oath worked to reinforce the sacral nature of the monarchy and its duty to protect the church.

Indeed, a few years later, as Louis XIV was about to embark on his 'personal' rule, he made a demand of his clergy that stands as a crowning achievement of the Bourbon monarchy. Though Jansenism had remained widespread in France, Pope Innocent X, under pressure from the Jesuits, had formally condemned its teaching in 1653. By 1661, therefore, Louis XIV was prepared to insist that all members of the French clergy sign a declaration accepting the papal bull. Many refused, and they were subsequently persecuted for it. By requiring the church to comply with his wishes in this way and to adopt doctrinal purity, as he saw it, Louis XIV was making a powerful statement about his spiritual authority and the nature of the monarchy. Like his father and grandfather, he would take his sacred duties seriously. Yet of these three Bourbon monarchs, he alone felt strong enough to demand both unqualified obedience from his subjects and respect of his legal right to impose a religious settlement which entirely satisfied his conscience and his obligations as king.

If the seventeenth century was a period of new scientific enquiry and rationality, as personified most famously by the mathematical and philosophical musings of René Descartes, or the writings of Peiresc, there is no evidence to suggest that by 1661 political authority had become secularised to any significant extent. Historians of France have a tendency to categorise too neatly the sixteenth and seventeenth centuries as ones of religious conflict and of political or institutional development respectively. Religion is credited as a motor of change in the social, political, and military development of the sixteenth century; whereas, the extent to which there was a political agenda to centralise and impose the authority of the state (the rise of absolutism) dominates writing of the seventeenth century. As a consequence, the consistent effort to build upon the compromise settlement of the Edict of Nantes and to fashion a reinvigorated, uniformly Catholic realm is played down. Certainly, Catholic reform can be viewed as part of a growing authoritarian trend in government in the seventeenth century. There was a determination by both Louis XIII and Louis XIV to direct reform and to maintain as close a control of the French church as possible. This created tension with many of their subjects and well-placed members of the church as well as spoiling relations with the papacy. Yet for the reform of the church to be effective, it would have to be undertaken at a 'root and branch' level, and this meant an unprecedented interference in the daily lives of its subjects. If the crown's authority appeared to be growing as a result, the desire to promote religious conformity and a single source of legal authority, all under the aegis of a strong king, was no innovation. The tripartite desire, often summed up in the formula 'une foi, une loi, un roi' (one faith, one law, one king), had long been the ambition of the French monarchy.

CHAPTER THREE

WAR

War was the principal vocation of kings. Defending their dynastic interests by force of arms was their defining role, just as it was the primary purpose of the state over which they ruled and of their governments. By extension, then, and for more obvious social and economic reasons, war had the most profound impact on French society. Despite the Peace of Vervins with Spain of 1598, Louis XIII never lost sight of the potential danger posed by France's traditional foe. Two branches of the Habsburg family held the extensive German empire and the Spanish crown along with its many possessions, including those overseas, and when the Thirty Years' War (1618–48) broke out in Germany between the Catholic emperor, Ferdinand II, and some of his Protestant princes (a conflict which also drew in the Protestant powers of the Dutch United Provinces, Sweden, and Denmark) fears in France grew of Habsburg hegemony in Europe. While the Peace of Westphalia of 1648 brought an end to the war in Germany (and secured Dutch independence from the Spanish crown), it did not end the separate conflict between France and Spain which dragged on until the Peace of the Pyrenees of 1659.

This extended conflict was both the making and the undoing of the reputations of Richelieu and Mazarin. In many traditional accounts, their determination to take the offensive against Spain was ultimately vindicated in the settlement. France had survived the Habsburg threat, secured modest territorial gains and crucially affirmed its relative status as the dominant military power in Europe, setting the stage for the pursuit of Louis XIV's growing military and political ambitions later in the century. More recently, historians have been concerned with the enormous cost of the war and the almost constant chorus of opposition to the cardinal-ministers that rang throughout the kingdom. This war presented many unprecedented organisational and financial difficulties for the French state and brought severe disruption and suffering to the people. There were few set-piece battles which could tip the military scales significantly, and it soon became a war of attrition that exhausted the treasuries of the two monarchies. Debate has centred around the extent to which the conduct of this war, and the fiscal and organisational pressures it brought, either strengthened or damaged the state. Often the cardinal-ministers are condemned by implication for pursuing a fruitless war at the expense of opportunities for the long-term institutional reform of the state.

There may be a temptation, therefore, for readers to conclude that it is impossible to identify a winner. The acquisition of Roussillon, Artois, and a few towns along the northern and eastern frontier was effectively the only tangible result from years of intense warfare. In other words, it might appear that at great cost France had achieved only slightly more than the *status quo ante*. Yet such a perspective ignores the priorities which those involved in the direction of the war themselves held. Neither minister pursued this struggle simply to secure a list of impressive territorial gains or for military posturing. Nor was the war fought for the material well-being of French subjects, even less as a way to centralise government surreptitiously or to expand the bureaucracy. For them, the purpose and motivation for conducting this war was only to serve the interests of their political master, the king. This service was, after all, the source of their own political standing and influence. Taking into account the crucial issues of the perceived 'justice' of the war effort, which never wavered, and the honour and reputation of the king, which was very well served by the final settlement, in every important respect this was a victory for France.

EARLY AIMS AND AMBITIONS

In his writings, Richelieu promoted his own reputation for being single-mindedly determined to make France a great power internationally. Perhaps the most obvious way to do this was to emulate the spectacular commercial successes of the English and especially of the Dutch. To some extent, the long struggle of the United Provinces for independence from the Spanish monarchy made them natural allies for France. On the other hand, from the perspective of the French ruling elite, the Dutch were something of an aberration to be disdained if not actually feared. The French nobility had little respect for a Protestant country with overtly republican ambitions run by, and in the interests of, mere merchants. At the same time, the Dutch could also arouse jealousy. They had a much smaller population and far fewer natural resources than France, and yet their coffers were being filled as quickly as their military influence was spreading across the globe. It is not surprising, therefore, that the principal instruments of this wealth and power, the trading companies, and in particular the Dutch East India Company, should attract the covetous glances of its traditionally more powerful neighbour to the south-west.

Many observers felt that, with a little bit of encouragement and direction from the government, France could easily compete. Accordingly, a number of fledgling French companies were also founded. By the time Richelieu came to the royal council in 1624, overseas trade was already seen as an appropriate instrument of French aggrandisement, and he wasted no time taking the initiative further. In 1626, he was named Grand-Master of Navigation and Commerce of France, a new position which replaced the old charge of Admiral of France. Under his auspices, other new companies were founded to encourage French trade around the world, as far away as Russia via Archangel in the north, in the Caribbean to the west, and in Madagascar in the Indian Ocean to the east. Perhaps the highest profile belonged to the Company of the 100 Associates in Brittany, which was given a monopoly of trade with New France, or Canada.

Although some merchants were unhappy with the 100 Associates' monopoly, this was a large company which, if successful, would have increased overall trade considerably. It clearly had another purpose too. The charter required the company to colonise New France with Catholic subjects and, by inference, to exclude Protestants. Thus the company was also an instrument of the crown's religious ambition to propagate the one, true faith. There were also clearly personal motives at work. As an investor, Richelieu, and his colleagues, stood to profit directly from the company's trade. As the founder, Richelieu's personal political authority in Brittany increased. For in addition to the monopoly on trade, it was also granted enormous privileges and freedom from government interference, both from Paris and at a local level. The direct influence in local affairs that this afforded Richelieu was far more effective than the severely restricted authority conferred by the titles of Admiral or even of Grand-Master. Thus this, and other trading companies, are effective representations of Richelieu's personal interest in, and dedication to, the reform and regeneration of France on a commercial, spiritual and even administrative level.

None of the companies enjoyed significant financial success, however, and none survived for very many years. It is tempting to conclude, therefore, that we will never know what would have become of Richelieu's reforming ambitions because his programme was derailed by war in 1627–28 against La Rochelle and, far more significantly, from 1635 against Spain. The financial and logistical demands of war, it is said, made internal reform impossible, and domestic issues were neglected. Yet such a conclusion draws a false distinction between commercial reform and war which clouds the greater, unifying ambition of his career: the need to back, with effective force, the king's dynastic interests. Certainly trade was useful in this regard in as much as it increased the crown's tax base, but companies such as the 100 Associates contributed even more directly to the crown's military strength. Their charters often required the founding of cannon for use at sea, the building of ships that were heavily armed and the availability of all of its resources for the crown in times of need. From the perspective of the crown, this was the priority and the main benefit of the companies.

Even the legal freedoms and direct authority of the cardinal-minister in the company's affairs were imposed, not to innovate with respect to local patterns of government and relations of power for its own sake, but to make it easier for the company to meet its obligations. So it seems that the varied motivations for founding the company were all subsumed by the greater ambition of meeting the crown's immediate strategic objectives (including any personal profit Richelieu might get which could be put to use in deploying forces on behalf of the crown). This is borne out by the events which quickly followed the foundation of the company in 1626. With the increasing threat of English naval intervention on behalf of the Huguenots of La Rochelle, Richelieu did all he could to build French naval strength, and a fleet from the Gulf of Morbihan, the company's base of operations, eventually played a leading role in cutting off the Rochelais' external support and in securing the royal victory of 1628.

From his earliest days on the royal council, therefore, war occupied Richelieu's attentions far more than commercial expansion or even domestic reform. Yet it was not just war with the Huguenots that concerned him. Indeed, Richelieu's initial foreign policy aims were directed against Habsburg Spain. Specifically, his attention was occupied by the aim of securing control of the Valtelline, a series of Swiss Alpine passes which would allow France to break lines of communication between Spain and its northern territories in the Netherlands and also provide a bridge for extending French influence into Italy. The opposition of the *dévots* was exacerbated by the fact that in November 1624 French troops in the Valtelline supported the local Protestant *Grisons*, who traditionally controlled the passes, and even defeated papal troops which had been sent to guarantee Catholic influence there. What unites the violently anti-Protestant domestic campaign against the Huguenots and this seeming anti-Catholic foreign policy against Spain is not unchecked militarism on Richelieu's part any more than it is his supposed religious confusion or indifference, but a consistent concern with the king's personal interests, both spiritual and dynastic. One could even stretch the point and suggest that protecting the very legal principle of divinely sanctioned dynastic inheritance itself was seen as the French crown's duty. As an illustration, late in 1627, French armies successfully backed the claim of a French noble, Charles of Gonzagua, Duke of Nevers, to succeed to the Italian duchies of Mantua and Montferrato. In 1629, they forced their way through the pass of Susa, which had been blocked by the Duke of Savoy, and successfully raised the siege of Casale in Montferrato, which had been under attack by Spanish forces. After occupying Casale, French military attention turned to Languedoc to extinguish the last remaining embers of Huguenot revolt there.

Although France enjoyed considerable military success in these years, its quick, successful incursion into Italy had not been undertaken lightly. It had been bound to attract greater attention by imperial forces, and indeed very soon Casale was besieged again. In 1629, with Richelieu in personal command of operations, French forces took advantage of an opportunity to take the fortress of Pinerolo in Piedmont. This was an important gain, yet on its own would never be enough to allow further French penetration into Italy or even the effective relief of Casale. Preventing Spanish or imperial dominance of Mantua and Montferrato, therefore, required a determined and sustained effort from the French crown to the point of occupying and controlling Savoy in order to protect supply routes. Compared with the rather lukewarm effort made at the time to colonise North America or to invigorate overseas trade generally, the enormous risk and the scale of operations undertaken to defend the dynastic interests of this French nobleman in a small duchy in northern Italy is striking. Even if one takes the view that Richelieu was only using Nevers and backing him cynically to extend the power of France abroad at the expense of the Habsburg emperor, who backed his own candidate, it must be assumed that such military intervention responded to far more deeply held priorities.

It has long been held that by 1630 Louis XIII was faced with the difficult choice between two basic policy emphases: reform at home or war abroad. In many accounts, Richelieu embodies the aggressive foreign policy option in opposition to the *dévot* Keeper of the Seals, Michel de Marillac, who preferred to pursue extensive reform measures designed to increase the state's finances and institutional strength. This tension was linked to growing resentment of Richelieu's personal influence at court and unease with the prospect of extended war against another Catholic power, which culminated in the greatest political triumph of his career on 11 November 1630, known as the Day of the Dupes. Many, including the Queen Mother, Marie de Medici, and the king's brother, Gaston d'Orléans, wanted the king to dismiss Richelieu. They became convinced that they would soon have their way, as, by all accounts, did Richelieu himself. Then in a dramatic and unexpected display of support, Louis XIII surprised everyone at court by choosing unequivocally to back his foreign policy and, by implication, Richelieu himself. His position as principal minister was consolidated, while the Queen Mother, Richelieu's former patron, was sent into exile. By choosing to support Richelieu, Louis XIII was effectively reconfirming that the crown's interests were best served by trying to check Spanish ambitions [*Docs* 13 and 14].

Yet it is anachronistic to suggest in this way that Louis XIII was weighing up two competing priorities, reform or war, for only the latter responded to his desires and ambitions as an early modern monarch. The debate in his mind leading up to the Day of the Dupes, such as it was, did not seriously countenance the abandonment of his foreign interests in favour of a programme to strengthen the state. Reform mattered only insofar as it might be necessary to improve the prospects of success. Thus questions were raised about political confidence in his servants and the practicalities of maintaining the current military commitments. These had become matters of some urgency, for in 1630 military fortunes had turned sour. Though French forces had secured most places in Piedmont, operations in Savoy itself had met with resistance. This made it difficult for France to provide any relief for Casale. Things looked especially bad in July when imperial forces took, and sacked, the initial focus of hostilities, Mantua, before moving west to reinforce their siege of Casale. This is the only reason the king may have been considering taking a cautious approach to war.

Despite these serious material and operational problems, Louis XIII had every reason to feel that he had made the right choice not to back Richelieu's political enemies. In October, France managed to get a small relief force to Casale, and the Emperor, newly distracted by Swedish successes in northern Germany, agreed to come to terms. Although French military fortunes had been decidedly mixed, the treaty signed in 1631 was a great political victory for Richelieu, for the terms had largely been set by France. Nevers was installed as the duke of Mantua, and Casale would remain garrisoned with French troops. France now enjoyed greater opportunities in Italy than ever. However, this success was a vindication not only of military preparations but also of dynastic planning. It was secured not just through strength of arms but by the subsequent death of the Duke of Savoy-Piedmont and the succession of his son, who was also Louis XIII's brother-in-law. This was not just a matter of good fortune. International relations at the time were conducted as often at the altar as they were on the battlefield. In this affair, Louis XIII's interests had been guaranteed in a very traditional manner, that is to say by a combination of long-term strategic marriages and timely births backed by the willing use of military force.

As with many other military campaigns of this time, this whole episode can seem rather pointless to a casual modern observer. There were few tangible gains for France to compensate for the enormous costs of the operations or for the suffering caused by an epidemic of plague which hit both sides very hard. Yet for the crown, defending dynastic rights was essential. By backing Nevers' legal claim, and by taking up arms to promote French interests, Louis XIII had successfully defended the honour, and enhanced the reputation, of the French crown, something that defined the very purpose of his role. It also reinforced the justness of his cause. To defend one's legal right to inherit territory did not simply provide the right, or an excuse, but a duty to fight. From Richelieu's perspective, then, the logistical and political difficulties involved in gathering an army strong enough, and the fact that fortunes could so easily have tipped the other way, did not suggest to him the danger or futility of war. Quite the contrary, it simply revealed how difficult, and indeed how important, it would be to maintain a determined stand to confront Habsburg power in the future.

With an eye to maintaining influence in the German Empire where the battles of the Thirty Years' War were raging, France also turned its military attention to the autonomous duchy of Lorraine on its eastern frontier and to strengthening its influence there. French armies intimidated Charles IV, the Duke of Lorraine, to guarantee safe passage of troops across his territory and to accept French 'protection'. Under increasing pressure and following a final incursion in 1633, Lorraine effectively became a possession of France. Although in this case France's approach was clearly crude and violent, even this was not an expression of naked territorial ambition, something unbecoming to early modern monarchs. Although French forces occupied Lorraine until 1659 with a brutality that was often shocking even by the standards of the time, the issue was not to incorporate Lorraine into a greater French state. Rather, the aim was simply to promote French interests abroad by providing access to the empire and the chance to offer plausible protection to German princes. As with French motives in Savoy and Italy, a strengthened position in a buffer state, it was hoped, would also help to defend France. There was another, more personal motivation too. Duke Charles IV's sympathies clearly leaned towards the Habsburgs. What is more, he openly conspired with Gaston d'Orléans, Louis XIII's brother and still heir presumptive to the French throne, who arranged to marry the duke's daughter, without the king's approval. Thus it was a combination of strategic considerations and an intolerable interference in French domestic affairs, indeed in Louis XIII's personal affairs, that led to military action. A French parlement, or judicial court, was established at Metz in 1633, which confirmed the legal jurisdiction of France in the area, but Lorraine was not annexed as such. The ducal crown was passed to Charles IV's brother, and once French concerns had been addressed, nothing further was done to limit Lorraine's independence constitutionally. Again, this had not been an opportunistic campaign by an instinctively expansionist regime, for pursuing these interests in Lorraine was risky, very expensive and thus required careful consideration. As would be expected, the occupation and further fighting there continued to drain valuable resources from the war effort elsewhere.

Events in the empire soon forced France to change its still relatively indirect approach to the war. For years, the Richelieu ministry had avoided open hostilities by supporting the Habsburgs' enemies with financial subsidies. This was a successful policy while the Swedish army under the command of King Gustavus Adolphus was enjoying great success in northern Germany. Although his death in 1632 probably came as good news to Richelieu, who feared too much independent Swedish success, the terrible rout suffered by the Swedish army at the hands of an imperial army at the battle of Nördlingen in September 1634, and the failings of the German Protestant Bernard of Saxe-Weimar, who was employed in French service, made it clear that the Protestant powers of Europe could no longer stand up to the Habsburgs alone, and France formally declared war in May 1635. As J. H. Elliott has suggested, far from being led into this war reluctantly by an aggressive, calculating minister, it was Louis XIII, not Richelieu, who was most determined to intervene directly, in spite of the evident dangers (Elliott, 1991: 117).

FRANCE IN THE THIRTY YEARS' WAR, 1635–48

France entered the Thirty Years' War against Spain hoping to establish quickly its military superiority in order to win a favourable settlement and end the conflict, though this soon proved impossible. After some early successes in the Spanish Netherlands in 1635, the French army suffered command and supply problems. In 1636, the tide turned decidedly against them. This year is often referred to as the 'year of Corbie', for Spanish forces advanced into north-eastern France as far south as the town of Corbie, about eighty miles from Paris itself, spreading alarm in the capital. The military situation was desperate, and the fear was real. Yet while France was able to concentrate its forces and repel the invading Spanish army, it is uncertain that Spain ever had any real intention of occupying Paris at all. It is far more likely that the Spanish forces were interested in occupying parts of northern France in order to extract contributions from the peasantry (so that the army would be able to pay for itself) and, if possible, eventually force France to sue for peace. This was not a war in which overthrowing the opposing regime was the objective. War aims in this period tended to be limited to securing the best possible negotiating position at peace talks. Neither Philip IV of Spain nor Louis XIII was interested in obliterating a divinely appointed rival who, it should not be forgotten, was also a brother-in-law. Nevertheless, Spain was clearly getting the upper hand in 1636 with invasion forces also in Burgundy and in some towns along the French Atlantic coast. In 1637, France began to lose further ground in Piedmont and in Alsace. Only in the south did the French enjoy any success. They finally pushed occupying Spanish forces from the Lérins islands, lying just off the Provençal coast, and they repelled an invasion force in Languedoc.

Suffering defeat in most other theatres, however, France attempted to take the offensive in 1638 with a bold invasion in the north of Spain, which began with the siege of the Basque port of Fuenterrabia. Richelieu had high hopes for this siege which was led by the Prince of Condé and the Duke of La Valette. The command was not orderly, however, and disputes arose, especially between La Valette and Sourdis, the commander of the navy which supplemented the landward siege. Though the fall of Fuenterrabia seemed almost certain at one point, the besieging French army was defeated by a relatively small and poorly organised Spanish relief force. Richelieu's anger and disappointment were palpable and, eager to protect his faithful servant Sourdis and his ally Condé, he made a scapegoat of La Valette and, by association, of his father the Duke of Épernon, governor of Guyenne, the political loyalty of both of whom Richelieu had been suspicious for some years. In this episode, we see a pattern emerging that was typical of the

Richelieu ministry. As the pressure on France mounted, and as French strategic objectives grew, so did the difficulties facing the commanders. French generals could expect to receive ever greater demands and consequently to be subject to near constant bullying and to have to shoulder full responsibility for any failures (Parrott, 2001).

The defeat at Fuenterrabia only increased Richelieu's determination to retake the initiative, both in Roussillon, a small province over the Mediterranean frontier with Spain, and especially in the Spanish Netherlands to the north east of France. Taking Hesdin and Arras in 1639 and 1640, the army under Richelieu's cousin, the Marshal of La Meilleraye, made good progress in Flanders. Yet because this was a heavily-fortified area, fighting was marked by long, drawn-out sieges which required enormous resources and manpower and, even when successful, progress was painfully slow. Moreover, these campaigns drained resources from other theatres. In 1640, rebellions in Catalonia and Portugal against the Spanish crown gave hope that there would be opportunities to intervene and take the war into Spain. While these rebellions undoubtedly helped the French war effort in the short run, they did not dramatically alter French fortunes. Indeed, perhaps the greatest immediate effect of the decision to concentrate forces in Roussillon in 1642 was a diversion of valuable resources from the north east and a fall in French fortunes on these fronts. Indeed, throughout this war, the effort to concentrate enough force to achieve a breakthrough in any one theatre of operations only ever seemed to come at the cost of failures in the others.

Neither Richelieu, who died in December 1642, nor Louis XIII, who died a few months later, lived to see the breakthrough for which they so longed. This came the following May when a large Spanish army invaded the Ardennes but was stopped at the battle of Rocroi by Louis II de Bourbon, Duke d'Enghien (son of the Prince of Condé, who later became prince himself, and is often known as 'the great Condé'). This was a clear French victory with as many as 8,000 Spanish dead and 7,000 prisoners. For this reason, Rocroi has been seen as the vindication of Richelieu's policies and is one of the most familiar battles of this period of French history. Yet for all its dramatic tactical success and the auspicious beginning to the new reign that it provided, Rocroi was not a significant strategic victory for France. It might have averted a disaster, but on its own it could not bring Spain any closer to surrender, and in this light it almost serves simply to make the greater war effort itself seem futile. This raises a number of interesting questions, not just about the motivation for continuing the struggle but more generally also about the changing nature of war and even of the emergence of the modern state, for military historians have tended to overlook the really quite limited political effect of such battles, instead seeing this period as one of dramatic military and political change.

For many years, the Thirty Years' War has attracted the attention of historians who have identified a 'military revolution' based upon a number of changes in tactics and military technology that were taking place mostly in western and northern Europe at this time. Above all, the increased use of light field artillery and the deployment of shallow, linear infantry formations which increased the fire-power and efficiency of musketeers, it is said, made war more offensive, decisive and much bigger. These changes required many more men, all of whom needed to be better trained and disciplined than before. Taken together, the effect was to make war not only more destructive but more expensive and difficult to direct. A debate still rages about the extent to which this pressure led to positive change and to the development of recognisably modern forms of government in Europe. It has long been held that France, as the emerging military giant in Europe, also experienced a military revolution of sorts. Certainly France had been unprepared for war in 1635, but after suffering some initial setbacks, Richelieu set out to reform the army and to put it on a sounder footing for the future, an effort that began to pay dividends at Rocroi in 1643.

David Parrott's work makes it clear, however, that France's conservative generals embraced these military changes with less enthusiasm than is credited to their European counterparts. There was no sudden improvement in tactics, training or discipline. Equally, far from rising to the fiscal challenges of the undeniably increased scale and cost of war with improved systems of taxation and organisation, the French government retreated from them. Although determined to maintain formal, royal control and not to allow private entrepreneurs to raise regiments of their own, as happened elsewhere in Europe, the French crown did not compensate its military officers for their relative lack of independence with greater financial support. Instead, more and more pressure was put on regimental commanders to advance their own money to keep their forces in the field. As the war progressed, it became harder to meet these demands, which undermined the effectiveness of the troops and the loyalty of their commanders. In other words, the administration of the army was not conducted according to any new organising principle or plan, but was characterised instead by inflexibility and weakness. Tremendous resources were poured into a war effort that brought little practical return.

Like armies elsewhere, the French army did grow considerably at this time. Late in the fifteenth century, the French had invaded Italy with at most 20,000 troops. By the 1690s, France would have an army of up to 350,000. The assumption has always been that in the intervening years there was a steady increase in the size of the army, punctuated by sudden leaps, especially after 1635. Despite the widely acknowledged problems involved with recruitment, poor pay and desertion, it is often assumed that the army under Richelieu reached as many as 200,000 men. Parrott has revealed the difficulties involved in making any such calculation of total army size. The matter is complicated by the number of different campaign theatres and by wild fluctuations in numbers. Nevertheless, it appears that France fell well short of its targets and rarely, if ever, had as many as 80,000 men in arms at any time. The significance of Parrott's work is not in the figures provided, however, but in demonstrating that the Richelieu ministry was not able to recruit anything like the number of troops it required to meet its strategic objectives and that, as the army grew in size, the government's ability to support and control it actually withered.

Since numbers of troops and the associated matters of logistics, supply and pay often determined the outcome of a battle, more than a new military tactic or technology, the implicit charge that Richelieu failed to rise to the challenge and to improve the administrative system is a serious one. From this perspective, it might appear that the traditional picture of Richelieu as a great state-builder is completely wrong, that he was, in fact, a rather poor minister, unaware of the nature of the problems he faced or simply unable to do anything about them. Yet this conclusion would be equally far from the mark, for his rise to power and his subsequent success at accumulating wealth and influence speaks of a political virtuosity and uncommon insight. Knowing with hindsight that far bigger armies would be raised and permanently maintained later in the century, it is easy to criticise Richelieu for his lack of imaginative reform to this end. It is harder, however, especially given the enormous pressures he was under, to imagine how he might have conducted this particular war more effectively. We should not lose sight of Richelieu's achievements in getting the best from a difficult situation and in surviving concerted political opposition and overcoming unprecedented financial diffi-culties to continue an arduous but honourable defence of the king's interests. One could argue that this very success obviated any pressing need for potentially disruptive fundamental reform of the state.

A problem for France (as for Spain) was that this war was fought on so many different fronts: on the north-eastern frontier with the Spanish Nether-lands, in Lorraine, the Franche-Comté, the Valtelline in Switzerland, northern Italy, the Provençal coast, the Atlantic frontier with Spain on the Bay of Biscay and later in Catalonia. With so many different theatres draining already over-stretched resources and complicating the administration, and command and supply operations, a lightning strike which would bring Spain to its knees was probably not a realistic possibility. Had this become an expensive and ultimately pointless struggle? For most contemporaries the answer was an emphatic 'no', for the king's honour and reputation remained at stake. Be that as it may, overall final victory could be achieved only when one side decided it was no longer possible to fight and to improve its hand at the negotiating table. This could be achieved only by grinding down the enemy's resources and will to fight in a long attritional war.

Louis XIII died just before the battle of Rocroi, and it was probably in part because of this victory and other recent successes that the fragile new regency of Anne of Austria could retain the recently appointed Mazarin on the council and pursue the same policy direction. French armies continued to push into the German Empire, and Henri de la Tour, Viscount of Turenne, one of the most gifted of French generals, who made his name in this war in conjunction with the Swedish army, was able to achieve what all armies of the time hoped to do. That is, he was able to enter foreign territory and extract contributions from the local population. This not only alleviated the burden from the royal treasury, it also denied the German Emperor the very same resources. At a time when finances and supply played such a large role in the success or failure of armies, this could make all the difference, and it undoubtedly played a role in bringing the Emperor to the bargaining table for negotiations which would eventually result, after five years of negotiation, in the Peace of Westphalia of 1648.

One of the most famous peace treaties in history, Westphalia is credited not just with ending the Thirty Years' War but with inaugurating a new era of international relations in which states recognised the integrity of international boundaries and the need to maintain a balance of power for collective security in Europe. Gone were the days of religiously motivated military interventions abroad, it is said. While there may be an element of truth to this, it is easily exaggerated, for the war which continued to rage between France and Spain differed in no noticeable way from the previous conflict and, more generally, early modern monarchs continued to be motivated primarily by dynastic interests and legal rights of inheritance, not by 'reason of state' or competition between coherent, modern nation states.

MAZARIN AND THE PEACE OF THE PYRENEES, 1648–59

French generals had won some dramatic victories in the 1640s. Along with Mazarin's diplomatic efforts, which helped bring the negotiations to a favourable close, on the surface, at least, things appeared to be going well for France in 1648. People could be forgiven for having thought that fighting was no longer necessary and for hoping that the fiscal and social burdens of the war would soon be lifted. Many, therefore, felt betrayed when the war with Spain continued and domestic strife only grew worse. For this, Mazarin has been blamed, and his reputation has never fully recovered. It should be remembered, however, that he faced a number of particular difficulties. As an Italian, Mazarin was a foreigner and an easy target for popular vitriol [*Doc. 25*]. What is worse, he began his ministry at a time of political turmoil. The new king, Louis XIV, would remain a minor until 1651, during which time the Queen Mother, Anne of Austria, would hold the reins of power, in his name, at the head of a regency council.

As had been demonstrated in the tumultuous years after the assassination of Henri IV in 1610, periods of regency government were often very difficult, with different political factions or individuals seizing the opportunity of royal weakness to vie for influence at court. Like Marie de Medici before her, Anne of Austria was distrusted as a woman, a foreigner, as well as for her close, some thought inappropriate, relationship with Mazarin. What made things even worse for them both was that Richelieu and Louis XIII had died in very quick succession. Not only had Richelieu's conduct of the war involved unprecedented taxation which bred hostility and resentment on its own, but in order to overcome any potential resistance Richelieu had governed with an iron fist. With a concern for political loyalty bordering on the paranoid, Richelieu had deliberately sought to disgrace or to isolate many otherwise powerful individuals or families. In this way, he compounded the feelings of resentment which the financial burdens of the war had caused. Once in office, therefore, Mazarin was faced with an especially volatile situation. Many previously ostracised, angry political voices competed to reassert themselves. This was a situation which would have been virtually impossible for anyone to manage effectively.

In such a vulnerable position, Mazarin's contemporaries, along with subsequent historians, have wondered why he chose not to take the opportunity to bask in the glory of Westphalia, withdraw from all conflict, return taxation to its pre-war rates, and work to ensure political stability at home. This might have been the easier route for him. The answer for most has been that Mazarin was personally motivated. He seemed to want military glory at almost any cost. Primarily, however, it is felt that through increasingly onerous taxation and corrupt war leadership he could amass a vast personal fortune while retaining political power. Although the conduct of the war was indeed the source of his unprecedented wealth, it should not be forgotten that it was also the source of nearly uninterrupted, unbearable political pressure that not only threatened his career, fortune, and social standing, but his very life. Thus a reasonable observer must also look elsewhere for answers to understand fully his motivation for continuing the war.

One important consideration is quite simple. Spain, no longer distracted by the long struggle with its rebellious Dutch subjects, saw an opportunity to gain ground on France and was not interested in signing a peace. From Mazarin's perspective, too, the matter was rather straightforward. Unlike Richelieu, he had inherited a war that was already raging. More to the point, the aims in this war had not yet been met: a position of military superiority from which favourable terms could be negotiated. It may seem to us, as outsiders, that a political opportunity had been wasted. Yet to end the war just for the sake of peace, or for political expediency, would have been difficult for Mazarin, because for both him and Richelieu the motivation for, and purpose of, war was the same. The honour and reputation of the crown could only be served with further fighting. Although the war in the German Empire was over in 1648, Mazarin did not take his eye off the prize of Italy or the main enemy, Spain. And later that year, the great Condé won another

major victory at Lens, in the Spanish Netherlands, which only further reinforced Mazarin's confidence that it was still worthwhile to pursue Spain.

Although things went dramatically wrong for France both domestically
and internationally after 1648, to be fair to Mazarin, at the time, internal
problems within the Spanish empire also seemed to suggest that France would
benefit, in relative terms, from a prolongation of hostilities. In 1642, French
fortunes in Italy had enjoyed an upturn. Certainly at sea things seemed to
be going France's way. In 1646, the important port of Dunkirk on the English
Channel was taken, which had been used by the Spanish crown for many
years as a base for disruptive privateering raids on enemy shipping in northern
waters and to put pressure on the Dutch rebels. Although a French attack that
year on the Italian port of Oribitello, on the island of Sardinia, descended into
a pointless and uncontrolled sack of the city, in 1647 an opportunity for
effective intervention in Italy arose with tax rebellions in Naples against the
Spanish crown. Another naval expedition was sent that year, and the French
commander, the Duke of Guise, was briefly proclaimed Duke of Naples.

From there, however, France did badly. Guise lost Naples in 1648. That
year, a French siege of Cremona in northern Italy was beaten back, and over
the next two years the French continued to lose influence in Italy. By 1652
things had turned from bad to worse: Dunkirk was retaken by Spain; Milanese
forces took Casale and Monferrato; and French troops capitulated in Barcelona.
Only a garrison at Pinerolo remained of the entire French experiment in Italy.
By 1657 French offensives in northern Italy had stopped completely. Despite
Mazarin's determined efforts to turn the situation around, he understood
by this time that to maintain people's grudging support for war taxation and
to get the edge on Spain, he would have to recognise, reluctantly, the new
republican government of England under the leadership of its Lord Protector,
Oliver Cromwell. An Anglo-French military alliance of that year made all the
difference. In 1658, a combined naval force attacked Dunkirk. This and a
series of other victories in the north led to the final negotiations and France's
relative position of strength.

The Peace of the Pyrenees of 1659 certainly favoured France, though
less by the territorial gains that were recognised than by the negotiations for
the marriage between Louis XIV and the Spanish princess, Maria-Theresa, the
daughter of King Philip IV. Such a high-profile marriage between the two
competing monarchies was not only a way of securing a lasting peace, but
it also satisfied the dynastic interests of the House of Bourbon. The marriage
was celebrated in 1660 at St Jean-de-Luz near the Pyrenean border with
Spain, and this was considered by contemporaries to have been the most
significant aspect of the settlement. Although his queen formally renounced
her claims to the Spanish throne, with this marriage Louis XIV was establishing
a potential future stake for his family. The following year a son and heir was
born, and years later, though it came at a considerable cost, Louis XIV

witnessed the fruition of all of his efforts when his grandson was recognised as the first Bourbon king of Spain in 1713, a prospect beyond the wildest imagination of any previous king of France.

Clearly by 1659 France had not defeated Spain decisively in battle. Nearly every account describes this war as a long struggle in which both sides lumbered towards a state of mutual exhaustion. It might be hard, therefore, for some people to see how the result could have justified the financial, political, and, above all, social sacrifices that were made. Yet from a contemporary perspective, France had clearly won, and few at court would have regretted the effort taken to this end. Had France simply capitulated earlier, Spain would certainly have imposed terms that the king and his first minister, and indeed many among the French elite, would have found unacceptable. In the event, along with its territorial gains, France had withstood whatever threat had been posed by the greatest power of the time, had emerged with its reputation and honour greatly enhanced, its international standing con-solidated, and the dynastic interests of the king well served, all at the expense of Spain. It is hard to think that in 1635 anyone realistically expected to achieve much more than this. By holding on as long as they had, in the face of considerable domestic turmoil, financial chaos and military reverses, the two cardinal-ministers earned the extraordinary confidence of their political masters for which they are famous, for in the process they helped satisfy the ambitions that had been held most dearly by the crown for a century and a half or more.

CHAPTER FOUR

GOVERNMENT

Open resistance to the crown was commonplace in the early modern period. The key to effective government, therefore, was the careful calibration of the response to this resistance. Indiscriminate, violent repression of rebellion, or even the repeated invocation of the crown's theoretically absolute authority to impose its legal will, could, in fact, have the unintended effect of enflaming further, potentially crippling, opposition. Some measure of sensitivity to grievances was required to guarantee the maintenance of sufficient co-operation from French subjects to continue the pursuit of greater political ends. This balance was particularly difficult to strike in the seventeenth century, when the increasing need for tax revenue to conduct the war with Spain led to rising resentment throughout society of the government and its increasingly heavy-handed methods. In this light, perhaps even greater than the test faced on the field of battle was that of maintaining the support and domestic stability necessary to keep the mobilisation for war practicable.

Throughout the seventeenth century, there were widespread and frequent popular rebellions against the government, a violence that speaks eloquently to the increasing suffering and desperation that was felt throughout the kingdom. Politically, the opposition to the cardinal-ministers was often intense, as witnessed by the number of conspiracies against them. During the Fronde, in particular, the chorus of discontent included the voices of the parlement, or judiciary, and others within government itself. This coalescence of the weak and the powerful, of common people, functionaries and nobles, all in opposition to the government, resulted in the potentially disastrous civil wars that characterised the years 1648 to 1653. The balance could very easily have tipped against Mazarin. Yet somehow in the face of intense opposition, the government survived and indeed prospered. It is easy, therefore, to see how this episode fits in historians' models of rising absolutism. By surviving a widespread rebellion, the theoretical foundations of monarchy were reinforced, and the government responded to the challenge with renewed vigour and modernising purpose.

Yet it is worth reminding ourselves that the government was largely responsible for arousing this opposition in the first place. It did this by pursuing, with such determination, the fundamental religious and military aims traditionally held by the monarchy in the past. That it was largely successful on both counts by 1661 suggests a continuity in approach that largely belies theories of modernisation or change. Certainly the size and sophistication of the machinery of government grew, and in some respects relations of power between the king and his subjects or his institutions were renegotiated. But these were incidental outcomes of this pursuit. The ability to overcome the spate of rebellions in the early seventeenth century, including the whole dangerous episode of the Fronde, emphatically confirms the appropriateness and effectiveness of existing methods of government. The success of the monarchy lies in the pragmatism and compromise that characterised these years of government and, above all, in the careful manipulation of networks of personal influence for support in the absence of modern, bureaucratic governing institutions.

POPULAR REBELLION

New or increased taxes were the immediate cause of most rebellions, whether those led by influential people with vested interests or by an increasingly straitened peasantry upon whom the burden mostly fell. From the 1620s, when the crown began raising taxes to meet its already spiralling military bills, France suffered nearly continuous resistance and often violent rebellion against the crown and its agents. There were as many as one thousand violent uprisings in the French countryside in the seventeenth century, most of which occurred prior to 1661. Specifically, from the moment France declared war on Spain in 1635, the financial pressure increased so rapidly that it led to what James Collins has called a 'twenty year crisis', climaxing with the troubles of the Fronde (Collins, 1995).

Many peasant rebellions were surprisingly well organised, widespread and threatening. Among the most remarkable are the two referred to derisorily after the footwear of the participants: the *nu-pieds* (barefoot) of Normandy in 1639, or the *croquants* (clodhoppers) in the south-west from 1635–37 which possibly involved as many as 20,000–30,000 peasants. The complicity of many local notables with the *nu-pieds* led the king, after suppressing the revolt with royal troops, temporarily to suspend the town council of Rouen and the provincial parlement there. Even though such large-scale armed rebellions could eventually be contained, they were symptomatic of a widespread discontent that could not be ignored and which threatened the crown's ability to continue to wage war. This constant threat of civil disobedience and armed resistance occupied much of the crown's energy and resources, especially as much of it came from the towns, where in many respects the stakes were much higher. William Beik provides an analysis of urban revolts in Dijon (1630), Bordeaux (1635) and Montpellier (1645) as but three among the more notable examples (Beik, 1997).

Although France remained a predominantly rural and agricultural society, on the whole its cities and towns were growing in size and in political and social significance. They never accounted for more than twenty per cent of the population, yet they had a disproportionate influence. This growth was uneven and occurred for a variety of reasons. Some cities grew from the effects of local commercial or industrial expansion. Others grew more directly as a result of the state's activities. New military bases or naval centres, and the investment required to support them, often led to urban transformations. Provincial capitals, or other administrative centres, also often witnessed growth which accompanied the expanding royal bureaucracy. The proliferation of religious houses in the seventeenth century contributed further with the increased concentration of clerics. Accompanying such changes was an increased attraction felt by the nobility, many of whom took up permanent residence in cities or built town houses.

It was not always easy for the crown to meddle in municipal affairs for the purposes of taxation. The organisation of urban government was incredibly complex, with each city having its own administrative structure. Some, such as Marseille, Bordeaux or La Rochelle (before 1628) were virtually independent of royal authority, enjoying a number of long-held privileges or tax exemptions enshrined in royal charters that sometimes extended back to the Middle Ages. Many communities, often (though not exclusively) those living near the frontiers of the kingdom, had relatively extensive and elaborate commercial networks and strong local identities. Traditions of citizen participation in government, for example, or the existence of local legal immunities, or simply valuable commercial interests, could bind together different groups in collective resistance, at least momentarily. With the poverty and squalor that was typical of early modern towns and the increasing burden of taxation by the state, by municipal government or by both, it is perhaps no great surprise that towns were often the epicentre of popular protest and revolt.

Popular anger was not constant or unfocused. Rather it tended to be sparked by a particular incident and directed against an individual, or set of individuals, who were seen to be responsible for causing distress, like a royally-appointed tax collector or indeed a local dignitary. Nevertheless, it was often furious and genuinely dangerous, part of what Beik refers to as a wider 'culture of retribution'. Urban magistrates or other local officials generally felt threatened by popular revolt and could be pressured to declare their solidarity with a movement while waiting for the anger to 'burn itself out' (Beik, 1997: 260). Active obstruction or violence might be ineffective or, worse, merely fan the flames of revolt. From the perspective of a provincial governor or of the crown, too, short of mounting expensive and logistically impractical campaigns against rebellious towns, it was often felt better to grant some temporary concession or to wait until the fury had passed.

Only much later in the century would local royal officials be strong enough to mobilise forces and to keep the potential for rebellion more or less under control militarily. Yet the incidence and nature of popular rebellion cannot be understood simply in terms of the crown's military capacity to suppress it. With hindsight, it seems clear how the crown was able to survive these rebellions with its authority intact. It came down to the fact that it was difficult for any armed rebellion to attract, and retain, all segments of society or to spread geographically. On the whole, the rebellions were conservative. That is to say that they were reactions against perceived innovations or intrusions into traditional privileges or ways of life. As a consequence, they tended to be localised and limited, rarely undertaken with revolutionary aims to overthrow the established order. Invariably, rebels declared themselves loyal subjects of the king but with a specific grievance, either against a new tax or a particular tax collector or, on a larger scale, even a minister of state and his policies [Doc. 16]. In other words, although there was often genuine anger, there was always an underlying obedience to the crown, or an acceptance of the nature of the political system, which ultimately limited the potential damage of any protest, including one as protracted and serious as the Fronde.

Even had the military means always been available to suppress revolt, its use would not necessarily have been the most effective way of securing the order and loyalty needed. Instead, the government sought to influence routine matters of local administration. Many cities saw their formal, legal privileges eroded during the seventeenth century in favour of more direct royal authority. From the perspective of the crown, however, the specific form of municipal government mattered far less than a guarantee of obedience, order and the smooth collection of taxes. Again, rather than pursuing a deliberate policy of subjugation and the imposition of administrative uniformity, the state tended to rely increasingly on narrow, local oligarchies, or one local faction, whose loyalty it could thereby guarantee, over another. This is where the clientage networks of ministers could be useful. For example, in Marseille, there were lingering internal divisions from the sixteenth-century civil wars which made it an extremely difficult, potentially volatile city for the crown to control. Yet, despite a tax revolt in 1634, Richelieu was largely able to maintain his influence there by favouring a leading, local family, the Valbelle. After Richelieu's death, the provincial governor of Provence, the Count of Alais, tried to control municipal politics by appointing and supporting opponents of the Valbelle, but with only moderate success. The following years were marked by anti-fiscal riots inextricably mixed with the bitter and confrontational local political divisions. Thus, as Richelieu's ministry demonstrated, the demands of the crown were generally modest. It would be satisfied with the loyalty of a town or a province if its demands for taxation could be met. And it was in raising taxes that most of its efforts lay.

MONEY

The government resorted to a number of sometimes desperate strategies to try to increase revenue. In addition to raising taxes, it borrowed money on a colossal scale. At times, it insisted on 'forced loans' from a municipal government or other body. But this had limited potential, for it was not the best way to guarantee continued co-operation. Money was most often borrowed in a more conventional way. An established practice was to sell *rentes* to individuals, which were effectively bonds guaranteed against a particular revenue. The most common was the *rentes sur l'hôtel de ville de Paris* whereby an initial payment provided an investor with an annual dividend secured by the revenue that went to the municipal council. This was, in effect, a type of loan. People gave money, up front, to the government in exchange for future interest payments. With this, as with other expedients, the priority, it seems, was to get as much money as possible immediately, even if that meant mortgaging future revenue on unfavourable terms.

For this same reason, greater use was made of tax farmers, and of bigger tax farms, that is when a number of taxes were consolidated and auctioned off together. This way, the government could get its hands on a set amount of money, without delay and without risk. With such a system, the financiers, those people with the money to lend to, or to invest in, the government, or to bid for the privilege of collecting taxes, had an increasingly important, but ambiguous, relationship with government. While the financial machinery of government was relatively large, it was still too small to impose a coherent, nationwide system of taxation and redistribution bound by strict rules of transparency and accountability. Indeed, so far was the state from such a system that creating one was never given any serious consideration. Certain innovations might be attempted when it was felt necessary, such as the introduction of a new tax or even just the strict application of existing legislation. Yet the crown had to tread lightly so as not to provoke resistance or even open tax rebellion. The process of extracting wealth to support the activities of the state remained an inefficient, clumsy combination of authority, or force, and desperate pleading. To keep sufficient money flowing, corruption had to be accepted as a necessary part of financial management. Often it was known that local officials were mis-directing money, but it seemed that intervention might simply result in disruption and ultimately less money. In such cases, a blind eye might be turned. Normally, the activities of the financial officers were policed only nominally, yet in theory at least the crown had the authority to intervene with the *chambres de justice*, legal investigations into the practices and the accounts of suspect financiers or officers. This was an effective method of recovering money and at the same time of appearing to be doing something about corruption. Yet it was a device that would only be used sparingly thereafter, for it did the government no favours to appear to be harsh and uncompromising to the very people upon whom it depended. Certainly financiers and tax collectors were almost universally despised, not just for their sometimes brutal efforts to collect money but for holding the crown to ransom with extortionate rates of interest. Yet insisting on the eradication of corruption would mean jailing virtually anyone with the money the crown needed to borrow. The motivation and self-interest of money gatherers was often the most effective fiscal tool for the government at a local level.

In essence, the government was a war machine fuelled by a limited and intermittent supply of money from self-interested financiers and oiled by the local political influence and personal financial clout of its administrators. In this respect, one of the most important insights into the practical workings of seventeenth-century government has come from the work of Françoise Bayard, Joseph Bergin and Daniel Dessert on the way the private fortunes of Richelieu and Mazarin were accumulated and manipulated and on this hidden world of money dealers with influence on the government. It was clear to observers that, just as Sully had done, Richelieu and then Mazarin had become fabulously wealthy from the fruits of office. Many accusations were hurled at them, and at times it seemed that the argument that their personal grandeur was built at the expense of the state would carry the day and bring about their political downfall. Yet both Richelieu and Mazarin enjoyed the support of their monarchs and there could never have been any question of investigating their finances, largely because the state depended on their wealth and personal influence. Visible displays of opulence and power were part of the process of establishing political credibility, credit worthiness and influence within the relatively small world of financiers which allowed the government to function in these desperate times. In this respect, the distinction between private and public finance was blurred. Richelieu and Mazarin were not bureaucratic administrators of a discrete department for finance, as we would expect today. Instead, they were big financial players in their own right, working to enrich themselves and on behalf of the crown in what Daniel Dessert has called 'un système fisco-financier' (Dessert, 1984).

OFFICERS OF THE CROWN

The most unusual source of money, and the next greatest after taxation, was venality, or the sale of offices. In order to raise funds, the government could create a post in the legal or financial administration and 'auction' it to the highest bidder. Ambitious men would invest in government service in this way, not just to guarantee an annual salary, but to advance their careers and their social standing through service to the king. Depending on the status of the post held, families from financial or legal backgrounds could eventually become ennobled. This seemed a perfectly normal practice at the time, and people quite respectably bought and sold offices as they would other personal property.

With the greater demands occasioned by war, the bureaucracy needed to grow and venality met this need. That said, however, the French administration arguably grew unnecessarily large and remained inefficient. Clearly, the crown's motivation for selling offices was simply to raise money, and this was just another way of borrowing. There had already been a long tradition of venality in France, but in the 1630s and 1640s offices were sold at an alarming rate. The size of the administration ballooned with offices as important as judge down to local dog-catcher being created and put up for sale. Often existing offices were simply duplicated and sold to another person who was told to exercise the function of the office with the original holder in alternating years. In some cases, up to five different people could hold the same office. Naturally, this created resentment among those who saw the value of their investment suddenly fall in this way. But such was the thirst for office that the government was usually able to get away with it.

Since so much money was raised through venality, the crown became dependent on it, unable to consider seriously any attempt to stop the process or to buy back any substantial number of offices. One historian has called the government's chronic dependence on income from venality a peculiarly French 'disease' (Doyle, 1996). And rather than correcting the system and its abuses, the government only thought of more offices to sell and more ways of making money from it. One, introduced by Sully in 1604, was to accept an annual fee, known as the *paulette*, which an office-holder could pay each year in order to guarantee the right to bequeath the office after his death. By making offices of government inheritable, the *paulette* made it more difficult for the crown to control appointments, yet people's desire to have greater ownership of them made this an important source of revenue.

Although there is much weight to the argument that the crown was opening its government to self-serving, potentially unworthy individuals in this way, it is wrong to conclude that it was actively damaging its authority and rushing headlong towards the inevitable trouble of the Fronde. It must be remembered that, when an office was purchased, that investment was best protected by the purchaser through good service to the crown (which was theoretically in a position to purchase it back if necessary, after all). The people who bought these offices were hoping to participate in, and benefit from, the business of government, not to obstruct or redefine it. In an age when the concept of a meritocracy was unknown and there were few ways of demonstrating one's professional worth, venality actually recruited the wealthiest, most successful and ambitious elements of society. There were dangers with venality, of course, not least because future revenue was being mortgaged for immediate investment, but it not only brought in a great deal of money when it was needed most, but, in general, it recruited the able to government service at a time when the size of the administration was growing.

Whereas selling offices has been seen by some historians as an abuse, or the actions of a negligent and short-sighted crown compounding its long-term difficulties out of financial desperation, the widespread use of *intendants*, on the other hand, has been seen as a clear sign of the crown's positive attempts at reform, to impose order on the administrative system and to increase its direct authority, that is to say to modernise royal government. As the existing tax-raising officials proved incapable of meeting the enormous demand for revenue, the government resorted increasingly in the 1630s to the granting of special commissions to these trusted individuals. *Intendants*, either assigned to a province or to a specific army, were commissioned directly by the Paris government for a specific task, which was often the usual responsibility of existing local officers or institutions. The roles ascribed to *intendants* are impressive: it was their job, among other things, to ensure the efficient organisation of armies, to watch royal officials and to report on them to the government, to eliminate corruption, to supervise the levy of taxes, and to stamp out local rebellion. In effect, they were to be a direct expression of royal authority in the localities and, in this way, could over-ride the complex web of existing interests and institutions to some extent. In effect, a new, efficient administration was being erected to parallel and to overcome the weaknesses of the official bureaucracy.

The use of *intendants* undoubtedly brought some stability to government prior to 1648, and their role became increasingly formalised as the crown grew dependent on them. Yet it is hard to see the introduction of *intendants* as anything but another administrative expedient in reaction to immediate, pressing needs. The government did sometimes give extraordinary protection to them. Some provincial governors who did not get along with an *intendant*, for example, were moved to another province. Yet the intention does not seem to have been to disregard existing structures of power or to try to supersede them, and one must be careful not to exaggerate the wonders that they were able to perform. With only one or two per region or province, and a total number for the kingdom that never exceeded thirty-two, often sent on unpopular missions, it is very difficult to imagine how they could ever have been thought to have displaced the power of existing elites and institutions. In practice, even the *intendants*, as useful as they proved to the government, had to be careful. They had to be sensitive to local interests and in many cases actually to co-operate with existing powers. In other words, they had to play a difficult balancing act, directly representing royal authority and, in order to be effective, co-operating to some extent with the local elites. If their regular use as instruments of direct royal authority represents a substantial step forward for the crown, it is at least equally clear that there had been no deliberate plan to subvert traditional constitutional structures for its own sake. Any long-term increase in royal power they may have engendered was entirely incidental to the specific tasks for which they were commissioned. And in this light, by relying on *intendants* the government revealed much the same tendencies as with other royal initiatives of the time. That is, they were a practical, pragmatic means to an immediate end. When the crown felt it needed to rely on the direct personal interference of these individuals to exercise its authority, it was acting irrespective of established institutions and traditional office holders, not in opposition to them.

FRONDE OF THE PARLEMENT, 1648–49

Following the deaths of Richelieu and Louis XIII in December 1642 and May 1643 respectively, the usual political problems associated with royal minorities were compounded by the unprecedented strength of Richelieu's grasp of the politics and finances of the state and by its sudden relaxation. Mazarin had been chosen to succeed Richelieu, but not everyone was willing to transfer political loyalty to him. It would prove very difficult indeed for anyone else to manage the extensive network of Richelieu's personal clients which had saturated the political system along with the many who had felt aggrieved and were now eager to re-establish what they saw as their rightful place of influence in society. Compounding this political danger was the dire financial situation Mazarin inherited. Royal revenues had already been mortgaged two years into the future, and many parts of France were resisting paying any tax at all. Ironically, military successes, especially that of Rocroi just days after Louis XIII's death, raised the naive expectation that the burden of war taxes would soon be relieved. With these hopes dashed, it is perhaps remarkable that it took five more years before the government faced serious political rebellion.

The first phase of the Fronde, known as the *fronde parlementaire* (1648–49) after the Parisian parlementarians and other office holders who led it, was the direct result of many years of dissatisfaction with the financial policies of the government. The introduction and expansion of the *intendants* in the 1630s probably did the most to alienate established office-holders, for they saw in these royal commissioners a direct threat to their authority and thus to the value of the office in which they had invested. In 1642, for example, the powers of the *intendants* in the provinces had been increased to allow them to make tax assessments and then to farm the collection out to private financiers. At the same time, the annual salaries of the established officers was substantially reduced. This twin attack on the position of the officers bred considerable resentment. The spark which ignited the Fronde, on 18 January 1648, however, was the regency government's forced registration of seven unpopular edicts in the parlement by way of a *lit de justice*. This heavy-handedness led to protests from the parlement, which tried to amend the edicts. When the government responded by threatening to alter the terms of the coveted *paulette,* opposition to the government in Paris galvanised. The sovereign courts of Paris, which included the parlement, the Chamber of Accounts and others, decided in May to send deputies to meet in the *Chambre St Louis* to discuss fiscal issues and to plan their response. Although the government declared the meeting illegal, it still received from it a list of twenty-seven demands, including the abolition of *intendants,* the routine renewal of the *paulette* on favourable terms, the recognition of royal commitments to the office-holders, the overall reduction of taxes and the immediate dismissal of the hated finance minister Particelli d'Emery, another Italian. The parlement also demanded a greater role in government by insisting on the right to approve new taxes or the creation of new offices and a certain jurisdiction over royal finances. Specifically, it launched proceedings against three tax farmers. While the government attempted to defuse the situation with some conciliatory words and promises to reform, the parlement went ahead and implemented the full force of their proposals, also declaring that any new tax not registered by them was, henceforth, to be considered invalid.

In this atmosphere of open fiscal defiance, the crown's tax-raising capacity collapsed, as did its credit. With no one willing to lend and with little means of paying back the massive outstanding loans, the crown was virtually bankrupted. Some opposition leaders, most notably Jean-François Paul de Gondi (who was soon to become the Cardinal of Retz), coveted Mazarin's position of principal minister. In August 1648, the government took action against what it saw as this intolerable disruption to the financial administration of the war effort and open challenge to the authority of the crown. Hoping to capitalise on the good news of the royal victory by Condé against the Spanish at Lens, the government arrested two popular leaders of the parlementary opposition. This was an ill-advised tactic, however, for by having opposed taxes the parlement had built up a great deal of support from the people of Paris. Rioting ensued, and from 26 to 28 August the streets of Paris were barricaded by protesters. By October, the government was forced to concede to almost all of the demands of the *chambre St Louis,* including the removal of *intendants* from all but six frontier provinces.

Mazarin had no intention, however, of honouring this humiliating agreement. He was simply buying time in order to prepare the government's military response to this insurrection. Early in January 1649, the royal court left Paris for a second time and declared its intention to be obeyed. When the parlement, in turn, ordered Mazarin's expulsion from the country, it also began preparations for the military backlash from the government that it now expected. Three powerful nobles, whose names are inextricably associated with the Fronde – the Prince of Conti and the Dukes of Longueville and of Beaufort – helped to raise troops and organise the city's resistance.

Condé led a royal army to besiege Paris and to beat it into obedience, but the situation was now getting worse for the government. This campaign was indecisive, and the Fronde had already begun to spread to the provinces, especially to Normandy and Provence. Moreover, the parlement was negotiating support from Spain, and there were now rumours that Turenne might actually use his army to support the city [*Doc.* 26]. The government was forced to concede again, and on 12 March 1649 the Peace of Rueil brought this first phase of the Fronde to a close. Although essentially a compromise which did not satisfy all of the *frondeurs*, the peace more or less confirmed the reforms of the *chambre St Louis* and represented a considerable concession to the parlementarians who had been leading the opposition.

The stand taken by the parlement had clearly tapped into widespread discontent and in the summer of 1649, despite the Peace of Rueil, opposition continued to grow. There were other problems which compounded these dangers. From 1648, the French people suffered from poor harvests, high prices and also from bouts of the plague. To make matters worse, royal authority in the provinces had virtually collapsed by 1649. Royal tax collectors were routinely being ignored or even overpowered, often with the open connivance of local nobles or municipal governments. In this atmosphere, many people took the opportunity to express other grievances and to play out local tensions. The most troublesome places were Normandy, Guyenne and Provence. In Provence, for example, there had been longstanding tension between the royal governor, the Count of Alais, and the local parlement at Aix which erupted in virtual civil war in 1648. Thus despite the concessions extracted from the government, the violence of the Fronde continued to escalate.

What made the Fronde especially dangerous is that at some point all levels of French society were involved in legal, sometimes ideological and often open military opposition to the government. The period is characterised by an outpouring of intense personal hatred for Mazarin and the Queen Mother expressed in a flood of pamphlets and posters, known collectively as the *Mazarinades* [*Docs* 28 and 30]. These were distinctive for their colourful denunciations of Mazarin, certainly, but also ominous because of the depth of popular dissatisfaction they expressed. To those in government at the time, there was no reason to assume that France was in any way immune from the same regicidal and republican forces that had sprung forth from the nearly contemporaneous English Civil War.

For this reason, historians have spent a great deal of time considering the implications of the conflict between parlement and the crown. Some have seen in these protests the stirrings of a proto-revolution (Madelin, 1931). Only slightly more plausibly, it has been presented as a determined stand against an emerging absolutist government based on a passionate defence of sound legal principles of limited, constitutional monarchy (Doolin, 1935). Writing in 1954, Kossman played down the revolutionary intentions of the Fronde. There was very little that could be called revolutionary in the demands of the leading parlementarians (Kossmann, 1954). No one expressed opposition to the system of divine-right monarchy, as such, nor did they propose a truly radical programme of fundamental reform. More recently, A. Lloyd Moote has argued that this 'revolt of the judges' was a measured, but nevertheless very serious, reaction to the intrusive and disruptive policies of the crown which for some years had been eroding the privileges of the office-holders. There may not have been any genuinely revolutionary intent, but their stand did deter increasingly authoritarian measures by the crown (Moote, 1971). Indeed, although the monarchy survived in France, Orest Ranum has similarly warned us against judging rebellious movements by their long-term constitutional impact alone. The parlement had not just demanded significant reform but had succeeded in wresting important concessions from the government. The very fact that Paris had to be besieged by royal forces and that the collection of taxes was virtually suspended, temporarily bringing the government to its knees, is witness not just to the parlement's grave intentions but to its practical achievements as well (Ranum, 1993).

Nevertheless, because relations had soured to such an extent by 1649, it is easy to lose sight of the fact that the crown and the parlement were not natural adversaries but also partners. Certainly Richelieu had been heavy-handed with the parlement, by-passing them when he could on important issues or applying pressure on them to come into line. During the Fronde, there were undoubtedly serious innovations and demands that parlementarians would have found unbearable. And in these conflicts the government invoked the king's legal authority and the over-riding urgency of foreign war, while the parlement in turn defended the importance of its traditional constitutional role. Parlements had long ago been granted a special privilege of remonstrance, that is to say to offer reflections, even criticisms, of legislation on legal grounds. In practice, they had often been able to defer registration. In this way, the parlement had a plausible claim to be the defender of the constitutional interests and traditions of the state, and it wished to enhance this role. Yet it was in no one's interest to push these positions to their logical extremes. Conflict, or disagreement, between the crown and its parlements, provincial estates or any other body certainly occurred, sometimes over serious matters of jurisdiction. But it was accepted as a natural part of government, just as sometimes heated parliamentary debate is today. Though the crown found the traditional institutions of the state, in particular the parlement, to be a serious obstruction on occasion, no purpose could be served by its systematic reduction.

For the crown, granting the Peace of Rueil in March 1649 was a humiliating concession to the demands of the parlement, but at the time this was the least of its worries, for Turenne had joined the *frondeurs* in the meantime and was leading a Spanish army against France from the north. As for the parlementarians, they could not sustain a conviction for fundamental change.

A few years later, in October 1652, as opposition was beginning to wane, Louis XIV famously ordered the parlement never again to stray beyond the formal limits of its powers. It was to register royal edicts simply on the grounds that they expressed the royal will. On the surface, this apparent emasculation of the parlement seems to be a victory for a centralising, increasingly authoritarian government. Yet it masks a continuing, potentially dangerous, tension between the parlement and the still financially desperate ministry of Cardinal Mazarin. In the post-Fronde years, he did not try to interfere unnecessarily (Hamscher, 1976). There was a mutual, if very delicate, respect and working arrangement.

This reconciliation, as far as it went, was a sign neither of a government haunted by the recent events of the Fronde and afraid of reawakening the wrath of is office-holders, nor of a parlement that had had its ambitions defeated and was now meekly accepting its newly restricted constitutional role. To a large extent, it was a resumption of the natural order and of the delicate balance of interests within government. More simply, this suited everyone involved and served their personal interests. The *frondeurs* may well have felt the positions they had adopted were just and that the defence of the established order, as they saw it, was good for France. But they had also been defending their own positions within the state which they had earned or bought. What had made the government's policies intolerable was not necessarily the presumption of any additional legal authority, nor was it the financial strain they put on the general population. It was the devaluation of their investment in offices. Positions within the judiciary and administration were personal investments intended to protect the long-term financial and social interests of families. Although the gradual erosion of the jurisdiction and influence of an office and even the annual return from it could grudgingly be accepted, when it seemed that the capital value of the investment itself was being challenged too, this had been too much for many office-holders.

This is not to suggest that the parlementarians were indifferent to their institution, its role, its traditions and its jurisdiction. Indeed, they made some extraordinary demands in the course of the conflict and their continued opposition to the fiscal practices of Mazarin was vociferous, but the underlying purpose of their determined, armed struggle had not been to redefine the constitutional role of the parlement, but to guarantee their personal security, family interests and participation in the business of government. The wishes of the crown had been equally prosaic: the stability and co-operation to allow it to get on with conducting the war.

PERSONAL GOVERNMENT

Although the Fronde of the parlement had posed immediate dangers and had wrested concessions, it petered out because of a lack of national cohesion and ideological conviction. As Richard Bonney has pointed out, in particular there was a lack of religious conviction fuelling it. Morover, the various provincial manifestations of the Fronde had their own local interests in sight, and they could not unite into a national protest movement, certainly not one that could overcome the latent loyalty to the institution of monarchy and the recognition of the crown's fundamental right to make law (Bonney, 1980). Yet it would be unfair to both sides of the conflict to explain the events of the Fronde in negative terms alone, that is to say as simply the effect of a lack of cohesion and weakness among the *frondeurs*. In particular, it obscures the resilience of the government and its methods, which relied only in part on the formal institutions of power like the parlement.

Though there was nothing like modern political parties in early-modern France with policy platforms and internal organisations, there had always been political factions at court. Most often these were built upon ties to an individual or a family rather than to any particular ideological conviction. Such personal ties were very powerful, and indeed it was only on the strength of these that government could really be effective beyond the immediate confines of the court. The crown needed powerful individuals who could manipulate relatives, family retainers or clients in key positions throughout the country and compete with existing networks of influence. The only realistic hope for this lay with the exercise of the authority it entrusted to Richelieu and Mazarin, or with others, and of the personal power and influence they accumulated.

From a modern perspective, early modern government was thoroughly corrupt, run on a system of patronage and nepotism on an unimaginable scale. From an early modern perspective, however, for the super-rich to peddle influence and to secure reliable clients in government posts through patronage in a self-perpetuating cycle of personal aggrandisement was natural, perfectly appropriate, and even beneficial to the state (if conducted in the name of the king), for political authority was not neatly delineated along clearly established and enforceable constitutionally-defined limits. It was personal and competitive. This was a volatile age, when loyalty and influence were often more important than talent or qualifications. While calls to depose Richelieu and Mazarin were sometimes deafening, their dedication to the service of their king and their political dexterity ensured their survival and continued royal patronage, just as this patronage enraged those it ostracised.

To be sure, at times, the resentment and infighting born of factional politics at court were damaging. But at others personal influence could be used to the advantage of the crown and was often one of the surest ways of ensuring the co-operation it needed to function. Henri IV, for example, whose experiences in the sixteenth-century Wars of Religion meant he was no stranger to the dangers of factional rivalry, was happy to allow his minister-favourite,

Sully, a certain political pre-eminence, knowing that in turn he would be able to rely on his influence. The power of Concini and Luynes can be similarly explained, though nothing approached the personal influence and authority of Cardinal Richelieu. During his lengthy ministerial career, Richelieu had built an unprecedented personal power base. This bred considerable resentment, and Louis XIII received a number of warnings about how dangerously powerful and independent Richelieu had become [*Doc. 15*]. As early as 1626, the Chalais conspiracy, led by many high-ranking nobles, sought to oust the cardinal from power, and as late as 1642 the Cinq-Mars affair, involving a young favourite of the king, attempted the same. Thus it must not be assumed that Richelieu's longevity was inevitable. Similarly, the most important political lesson Richelieu learned, and one which he never seems to have forgotten, was that his own position depended entirely upon the personal support of the king. Richelieu was certainly an impressive political figure, but it is also true that his political ascent had been permitted only because he exercised his authority in the king's name. Without Louis XIII's interest in Richelieu's success, his career would have ended with an abruptness that could well have outdone Sully's after the assassination of Henri IV.

This reliance on the personal influence of individuals in order to govern was not new to the monarchy, and it accounts in large measure for the deeply divided and often ruthless personal politics of the time, of which Richelieu was a polished practitioner. His early success at earning the king's trust was largely built on savage political attacks on people who he accused of tipping the balance between self-interest and dedicated service to the crown. La Vieuville, the leading influence in the royal council prior to 1626, was the first of Richelieu's targets to fall, but he did not stop there, aiming ever higher. Richelieu also ingratiated himself by identifying the dangers posed by such figures as the king's half-brother and governor of Brittany, the Duke of Vendôme. Not only had he been implicated in the Chalais conspiracy, but Vendôme was accused of orchestrating an English attack on a French fleet in port in Brittany. Stripped of the governorship of the province, Vendôme was eventually replaced by Richelieu himself in 1631. One powerful individual had been replaced by another as governor of Brittany. Thus there had been no institutional innovation to the government of the province. From the perspective of the king, however, he now had in place a servitor who had demonstrated nothing but loyalty. For the estates of Brittany, who had requested Richelieu as a successor to Vendôme, they now had a powerful individual well-placed to bring benefits to the province. For Richelieu, he had not only secured his primacy on the council but he exercised considerable direct, personal influence on the ground. During his career, the cardinal's authority continued to grow. Duke of Richelieu and of Fronsac, he also accumulated an impressive list of other governorships, many of which were in strategically important coastal towns.

It was only through such a combination of political office and personal power that he was able to overcome regional particularism and resistance to central authority as well as he did. Richelieu's influence was felt everywhere in government. He was able to place enough trusted clients, or 'creatures' (literally, political creations), in important positions and to overcome potentially damaging factional rivalries. From this perspective, political power was much more blunt than is often assumed from the complex and evolving array of formal governing institutions or might be implied from historians' debates about where sovereignty lay. For example, it was only as governor of Brittany that Richelieu was able to exert any real influence as Grand-Master of Navigation, a position which in theory should have given him automatic authority over the maritime affairs of the province. Richelieu consolidated his position in Brittany further by placing his relations in such key positions as governor of Brest and of Nantes. It seems that as far as Louis XIII was concerned, any distinction between Richelieu's personal interests and service to the state had faded. The one simply reinforced the other.

Richelieu's ministry was relatively successful at enforcing the royal will because it was pragmatic, recognising the importance of securing sufficient personal loyalty and co-operation. For example, in 1626 it was not only the charge of Admiral that was suppressed but that of Constable of France, a military position of enormous authority. This change is usually attributed to Richelieu and his plan to improve the administration of the navy and army, making them more accountable and modern by removing these dangerously powerful positions which could be held by potentially untrustworthy nobles. In practice, the suppression of the admiralty, as an illustration, merely opened the door to Richelieu to take on the same authority in his new guise as Grand-Master of Navigation. Certainly, Richelieu achieved more accountability and reliability in the navy (at least from his point of view). The idea that he modernised the administration of the navy, however, is a myth, for it operated largely through him and on the strength of his personal influence. The navy became dominated by members of his family or his clients. In this way, Richelieu was not only extending his influence but was also better able to co-ordinate the kingdom's naval resources. From virtually nothing at all, the navy grew into a standing fleet of thirty-eight purpose-built warships by 1636, and France was largely able to hold its own at war against Spain, traditionally the greatest naval power in Europe.

On the command of the army, however, a far larger, more prestigious and more crucial institution to the crown's interests, it was much harder to keep such a close grip. Initially, Richelieu had enormous influence over appointments to key military offices and to specific commands, ensuring that reliable servants were promoted to the exclusion, in particular, of members of rival households, such as the Vendôme, the Guise or the Montmorency. In this way, he was able to impose a relatively coherent command on the army. As the scale of the war effort grew after 1635, however, it became impossible for Richelieu to maintain his virtual monopoly of influence. There were limits to the number of people in his network of clients and thus to how far he could displace his rivals. As the demands on the army grew, more and more commands were given to those nobles clamouring for influence who were outside of Richelieu's political circle. As a result, the command structure became confused and the effectiveness of the army suffered (Parrott, 1992). This is not to imply the criticism that Richelieu had failed by not introducing loftier or more effective reforms. Indeed, given the entrenched interests in the army, relying on personal loyalty and kinship to displace political opposition was almost certainly the only option open and quite likely did the army more good than harm.

Such a system is likely to breed resentment among many people, however, and during the difficult period of Mazarin's ministry this only got worse. Since all of the current problems were down to the war with Spain and thus, it seemed, to Mazarin personally, the *frondeurs* wanted an end to hostilities and the removal of Mazarin from office. This common focus on Mazarin for all *frondeur* energy, perhaps the only point of common interest, helped to coalesce opposition from different elements of society. Everyone blamed him for the war and called for his downfall. Mazarin also provided a safe and easy target, for by focusing on him and his policies, the *frondeurs* could claim only to be rebelling against a corrupt and corrupting minister, not against the king himself. An obvious way to defuse the dangers of the Fronde by the crown, therefore, might seem to have been simply to dismiss Mazarin. There was a principled issue at stake, however. It was beneath the dignity of a king to negotiate with, and certainly to be seen to concede to the demands of, his subjects. Like Richelieu, Mazarin had become the most powerful agent of royal authority on the royal council. Sacking Mazarin and replacing him with a rival claimant would have simply opened the council to factional influence and undermined its role as an independent expression of the king's authority, something that had long been important to the Bourbon monarchy. In addition, since the authority of a French king was defined in large measure by his role as a warrior, undercutting the war effort in this way would have reflected very badly on him. More immediately, despite the near universal opposition to Mazarin, there were also grounds for thinking that the administration of the army was actually improving.

An effort had been made to make a more coherent, governable institution of the army. More commissioners and treasurers had been appointed, and significantly from 1635 *intendants d'armée*, that is intendants with specific responsibility for overseeing the organisation and support of armies, were used. These intendants answered directly to the secretary of state for war who was also given more authority over all military affairs at the expense of other ministers. In a sense, then, a more modern ministry for war was being created for secretaries Abel Servien (1630–36), Sublet de Noyers (1636–43) and especially for Michel Le Tellier (1643–77). The close personal tie of Servien and de Noyers with Richelieu himself suggests that this innovation had indeed also been an attempt to increase the cardinal's influence in the routine administration of the army through his clients. Under de Noyers, especially, the naming of *intendants* was often opposed by other ministers of state, or by bodies such as the *bureau de finances*, by the chancellor or by others who resented Richelieu or who wanted to influence appointments themselves.

After 1643, under Le Tellier, *intendants d'armée* came to be accepted and their authority within the military hierarchy grew. It is tempting to see the hand of a constitutionally ambitious monarchy in the increased use and improved control of the *intendants* and in the insistence of the crown to reintroduce them after surviving the protestations of the Fronde. Yet whatever improvement to administrative efficiency that this introduced was not the result of a move towards more modern, bureaucratic, accountable government but a positive entrenchment of the trend of depending upon personal government. As David Parrott suggests, Le Tellier enjoyed far more independence from Mazarin than de Noyers had from Richelieu (Parrott, 2001: 461). This left him free of much political opposition, and he was able to ensure that appointments were made of able people and, more significantly, of his extended family or personal clients. Le Tellier's personal domination of the *intendants* for the army did not make it possible for them to resolve all of the problems within the administrative structure, of course, but it did provide some coherence to this body of administrators, making them more effective. Thus in this respect, as ministerial control from the centre loosened after Richelieu's death, personal, family interests below the ministerial level were allowed to dominate day-to-day administration, and the business of government arguably became more effective.

The domination of Richelieu and Mazarin in seventeenth-century French politics can appear to reflect some important innovation in government. Yet it is really only confirmation of the fact that kings traditionally ruled through the co-operation and influence of individuals at all levels of government. Early modern government was personal. That is to say, it was dominated by personalities and networks of personal influence far more than by institutions or formal government office. This was universally understood and accepted. Thus it is clearly anachronistic to read into this period an attempt on the part of the government to introduce absolutism or any other modernising agenda. Equally, the opposition to the crown, as threatening as it often became, was ultimately self-interested and divided. Yet as an explanation for the crown's ability to survive the misfortunes that had converged by 1649, with Paris in open rebellion extracting wide-ranging concessions, this is incomplete, for it denies a longer-term positive role to the government. It was not pursuing an enlightened vision of statehood against determined opposition, yet neither was it simply groping in the dark unable to recognise or to respond to the challenges it faced. Although the limits of a system of government that relied on the extensive personal influence of individuals was being severely tested under Cardinal Mazarin, it is important not to lose sight of its ultimate success.

CHAPTER FIVE

SOCIAL ORDER

French kings craved social order. This meant they wished to see an end to peasant and urban rebellions, certainly. But, more than anything else, this order required normal relations with the nobility from which, it was assumed, stability throughout society would follow. It is true, as the 'Fronde of the Parlement' had shown, that the institutions of government could be obstructive. More often, however, they were useful. To make law, a king needed law courts to register and enforce it. To understand regional concerns and to receive subsidies, he needed the estates in the provinces where they were established. In a similar way, he relied on his other bodies and a raft of officials and bureaucrats for a variety of services. Yet all of these were merely practical tools of government. In this society, real power lay with the nobility, and it was only through them that it could be exercised fully, as reflected in the eagerness with which non-nobles who served the crown sought, and were often eventually awarded, ennoblement for their families. Members of the existing upper nobility either had their own, largely independent authority in an area which the crown could hope to exploit, such as the Condé family in Burgundy, or they could be awarded key roles, such as important commissions in the army or a provincial governorship. The importance of governors, in particular, to the effective exercise of the crown's authority is reflected in the quality of the people appointed, sometimes relations of the king himself. In this sense, the elevation and dependence upon Richelieu and Mazarin was merely an extension into the day-to-day administration of government of the same political instinct. It was through men of status and influence that the crown ruled.

Thus although royal authority was at a low ebb in the summer of 1649, and historians have correctly identified very real dangers posed, the Fronde was about to enter into a more destructive and violent phase as the leadership passed to Condé, arguably the most significant noble figure in the realm. This 'Fronde of the Nobles', as it is often known, was more serious from the crown's perspective precisely because it was led by members of the nobility, the key elements of its military and political power. Historically, civil uprisings became genuinely dangerous to the crown when they involved, or indeed were led, by nobles. Thus, despite the apparent radicalism of the revolt that had been led primarily by the parlements and their more far-reaching demands, this rebellion posed a graver challenge to the young King Louis XIV. Or, put differently, it could only be with the defeat of this noble rebellion in 1653, and the re-establishment of a mutually dependent relationship with the king's most significant subjects, that the immediate dangers posed by the Fronde could be said to have passed.

The dramatic confirmation of Louis XIV's authority, as king, over all of his subjects in 1653 has reinforced the assumption of historians that the nobility had been in terminal decline by the seventeenth century and that this spate of rebellions was its last, dying gasp as a significant force in French society (Salmon, 1981). However, this theory assumes not only that the nobility was a coherent, uniform class, but that it was under threat by natural economic decline, by the actions of either an avaricious crown or a rising, non-noble, bourgeois elite, or a combination of these factors. Yet none of this is true. Recent studies have shown that, in general, the nobility retained all of its influence and indeed many nobles did rather well financially in the seventeenth century, despite long-term, adverse economic conditions and rising costs. More significantly, their elevated status was universally accepted. The relative quiescence of the nobility after 1653 was a welcome return to a widely desired stability.

The family and career of Louis II de Bourbon, Prince de Condé, the victor at Rocroi in 1643, is especially illustrative of the undiminished, but nevertheless ambiguous, role of the nobility in France. The 'great Condé' was celebrated as the embodiment of all that was laudable about the nobility. Traditionally, nobility was conferred through military service to the crown. It was this historic role as a warrior-caste which defined their elite status and which still guaranteed them a central place in the affairs of the state, characterised as it was by warfare. Not only had this first prince of the blood been born into a position of exceptional privilege, but Condé's stature had been matched by equally remarkable military prowess and success on the field of battle. He had also been a patron of the arts. This was a reflection of the refinement demanded of the nobility who were expected to live a lifestyle of elegance and wealth befitting, and therefore reinforcing, their status. The very virtues that made him an ideal servant of the crown, however, also made him a potential danger. Like his ancestors in the sixteenth century, and his father who had led noble rebellions in the 1610s, the relationship between the 'great Condé' and the crown was transformed when he led the final stages of the Fronde. France's greatest living general was charged with treason and entered into Spanish service.

After the Fronde, Louis XIV was in a much stronger, more secure position than his grandfather, Henri IV, had been following the sixteenth-century civil wars. Yet both were magnanimous in victory towards the nobility. Though under no compulsion to do so, in 1660 Louis XIV pardoned Condé and re-embraced him as a significant, leading figure in French society, albeit a defeated and less dangerous one. That the king desired such an accommodation and that Condé felt no loss of dignity in coming to it, says a great deal about the reciprocal nature of the relationship between the Bourbon monarchy and its nobility and indeed of the nature of the seventeenth-century state based, as it largely was, on noble interests and a notion of noble virtue.

THE FRONDE OF THE NOBLES, 1650–53

The Duke d'Enghien, as the great Condé was then known, led the royal army that besieged Paris in 1649, arguably saving the government from a desperate, potentially fatal, situation. He had no respect for the parlementary demands of the early Fronde. There was no need for any constitutional change, as far as he was concerned. It was only his own growing personal grievance that led him later to take up the leadership of the rebel cause. As a reward for his earlier services, Condé felt he naturally deserved more power and influence in government. From the perspective of Anne of Austria and Mazarin, however, to give in to Condé's increasing demands would have been a political defeat and an abrogation of their responsibility to protect the independence and integrity of the crown.

To capitalise on, and also to reinforce, people's deep-seated loyalty to the monarchy and to protect themselves from Condé and other nobles who felt ostracised or otherwise aggrieved, the crown adopted a two-fold strategy. Between 1650 and 1652, Anne toured the kingdom with the young Louis XIV, visiting as many places as possible, presenting her son and playing on people's emotional responses to the presence of their king. More dramatically, in January 1650, they staged the arrest and imprisonment of the increasingly troublesome Condé and his brother, the prince of Conti, along with their brother-in-law, the Duke of Longueville, who was governor of Normandy. It is fair to say that the first strategy, at least, was a moderate success. The second, however, simply caused more resentment. The clients and relations of these troublesome men were not willing to go down without a fight, and they fomented resistance to the government in many parts of France. When the king's tour reached Bordeaux in August 1650, he found a particularly recalcitrant city that was already under siege by royal troops. Here it was the princess of Condé who was exploiting the almost universal animosity felt by all sections of local society (parlement, municipal government and people) against the government. Much of this hatred had been focused on the provincial governor, the second Duke of Épernon, who had been forced out of the province. By the end of September, the government negotiated the formal dismissal of Épernon in exchange for the city's surrender. Although the city opened its gates to the king, and to Anne and Mazarin, in October, this was not the end of the troubles there. The Fronde would flare up again and would continue at Bordeaux longer than anywhere else in France.

Bordeaux was exceptional, both for the success and longevity of its rebellion and for its far-reaching, almost egalitarian demands. There had been a history of rebellion there, most recently in 1635 when the imposition of a new tax on wine had led to a local uprising [*Doc.* 16]. During the Fronde, however, a radical bourgeois movement, known as the Ormée, rose up against the municipal government and the parlement of Guyenne and insinuated itself into power, eventually taking formal control of the city in June 1652 [*Docs* 31 and 32]. The Ormée secured its position, in part, by assuming control of the maritime traffic in the Gironde with a small navy and even by raising a modest army. As a radical movement, however, it eventually failed to unite the different elements of Bordelais society behind its increasingly radical political experiment, and by the beginning of August 1653 royal troops finally defeated and took the city.

Because of its unusual character, the Ormée of Bordeaux has attracted the interest of historians. Sal Westrich, writing in 1972, saw in it evidence of a radical class struggle (Westrich, 1972). Others have been careful to include the Ormée in accounts of the Fronde, but usually as an important footnote, either as an interesting exception to events elsewhere or as a hint that genuinely revolutionary tendencies may well have been at work, providing the Fronde with extra gravitas. Yet the threat the Ormée posed to the government was not in its genuinely radical agenda but in the intervention of Spanish forces which it invited on its behalf and, above all, the support it offered to Condé. Indeed, it was Condé who negotiated the arrival of a Spanish fleet in the Gironde in 1651 to defend Bordeaux from the French crown. Earlier in the year, many nobles and parlementarians had put pressure on the government, hoping to bring about Mazarin's downfall, replacing him in the royal council with Gaston d'Orléans, the king's uncle. Eventually relenting, Mazarin set Condé and the other prisoners free in February and fled into exile near Cologne, while the king and Queen Mother were kept under virtual house arrest in Paris.

For members of the high nobility to deal with a foreign monarch on an equal footing and invite military intervention in France, as Condé had in 1651, was rare and an extraordinarily bold move. Clearly, the nobility could wield enormous influence, though ultimately a lack of unity of purpose undermined the strength of their opposition. From his exile near Cologne, Mazarin tried to exploit divisions within the nobility. In particular, he tried to further isolate Condé, the most powerful and dangerous of them all. Through Anne, he bargained with Retz, whom Condé disliked, enticing him with the coveted cardinalate. By 7 September 1651, Louis XIV had reached the age of majority, and Condé's position was thoroughly undercut, for many people who had been willing to fight Mazarin, a foreign minister of state, were now unwilling to be seen to be in opposition to the direct authority of their legally constituted king. Though few people welcomed Mazarin's return to Paris that same month, most *frondeurs* such as Turenne saw no possible advantage to further resistance and returned to his side. Condé was forced to retreat to his stronghold of Bordeaux from where he would begin to conduct what could now only be interpreted as an open rebellion against the king.

Despite being declared guilty of treason, Condé remained defiant because he could not accept the way he had been marginalised. He also had the means to continue to fight, and in choosing to do so he could rely on the legal principle, however peculiar or flimsy it might seem to us today, that nobles, especially ones of his stature, had an historic and rightful place at the heart of political power in France. In addition to the military resources available in Guyenne, and the aid he negotiated from Spain, he also had the explicit political support of Bordeaux and the provincial parlement which still longed for a constitutional settlement that would favour them. In April 1652, Condé returned to Paris at the head of a rebel army. The aim was to join forces and to fight for control of the capital with Gaston d'Orléans, with whom he had negotiated a working arrangement, despite never having been close allies. With Turenne's royalist forces over-stretched, Condé entered the city to stir up popular rebellion, and by July it seemed he was successful. The Paris parlement declared Gaston and Condé the Lieutenant-General of France and commander of the army respectively.

This was a short-lived victory, however. Gaston had been an unpopular figurehead, especially among many of the parisian elites, and Condé, too, ultimately failed to overcome the reluctance of many to join his struggle. The lingering memory of his command of the royal forces that had besieged the city in 1649 no doubt played a role. Later, in July, Condé suffered a terrible defeat at the hands of Turenne on the outskirts of Paris, and this further weakened his grip on power. In the midst of this confusion, and in response to the apparent divisions among his opponents, Mazarin made a very shrewd move. He offered to go voluntarily into exile, again, and to remain out of government in exchange for the return of the king and the Queen Mother to full authority. This satisfied many people, including Gaston who made peace in October 1652, and *frondeur* resistance effectively collapsed. War-weariness and residual loyalty to the crown had ultimately undermined Condé's influence, and he retreated to join forces with his Spanish allies.

Louis XIV returned to Paris on 21 October. A *lit de justice* was held at the parlement at which a sort of amnesty was declared. Everything the parlement had declared during the disturbances was annulled. Many of the leading *frondeurs* were banished, and it was made explicit that the officers of the courts were never again to have independent dealings with noble families nor to meddle in affairs of state. Suppressed taxes were re-imposed; *intendants* were re-introduced; and other concessions forced by the *frondeurs* were reversed. Mazarin returned to Paris, and to office, in February 1653.

So profound had been the grievances of all sections of French society that it is tempting to assume that with this victory by the crown something significant had changed in French constitutional history, that a first significant step had been taken in the invigoration of a new-style monarchy. Yet this had been only a restoration, a confirmation of the king's legal authority. The immediate dangers might have passed, but none of the problems of the pre-Fronde years had. To conclude that royal authority had been restored in 1653 to some distant, historic ideal or that a new style of government, that could now be called 'absolute monarchy', had suddenly emerged is to ignore not just the on-going opposition to the government and the difficulties it continued to face in the war with Spain but the aims of those involved. Nobody had fought for fundamental reform of existing political relations of power. In other words, the thoroughness of the crown's victory speaks more plausibly to the fundamental unity of the constitutional purpose of everyone involved than to the success of any polarising agenda.

In the actions of the nobility who raised armies against the government there was undoubtedly an element of naked ambition and fractious self-interest at play, though their protest had been more than personal ambition and destructive pride run amok. As they saw it, the nobility, and the princes of the blood in particular, had been partly displaced by the cardinal-ministers, with their clients, who had upset the 'natural' distribution of political power. Just as with the office-holders who, despite their apparently more radical demands, had been unhappy with being progressively excluded and who wished for a restoration of their positions within government, the nobility wanted to retain its influence within a traditional, royal government. Equally, from the crown's side, it had not been actively working to exclude either group from power. It, too, had been fighting for the restoration of good government, in which nobles, office-holders and traditional institutions of state worked together for the greater glory of France. The Fronde had been a battle in which all of the contestants sought a restoration of the natural order, as they saw it, and virtually everyone agreed that it was to be headed by a strong monarch.

LOUIS XIII AND THE NOBILITY

Towards the end of his life, Cardinal Richelieu compiled a number of documents and personal reflections. Ostensibly this *testament politique*, which contained maxims and principles of government, was intended as a guide for Louis XIII after Richelieu's death. It was also, quite clearly, a reflection on his career as principal minister and a celebration of his contribution to the state. The most intriguing boast is that Richelieu had succeeded in taming the pride of the nobility on behalf of the crown. Over the centuries, the *testament politique* has been very influential with historians and this rather unlikely-sounding claim, in particular, has helped to feed the idea that the nobility were an obstacle to the ambitions of the crown [*Doc. 24*].

Richelieu's relationship with the nobility, however, was far more complex than this picture would allow. There were certainly many individual nobles who incurred his wrath and were forced out of office, into rebellion or even eventually into exile and who could reinforce his claim. Yet far from being an enemy of the nobility, Richelieu was, of course, a noble himself and an extraordinarily successful one at that. As we have seen, Richelieu did not operate so much as a modern bureaucrat but as a personal power broker, and he relied on the influence of other nobles or other local elites to be successful.

Richelieu was certainly keen to present himself in the best possible light in the *testament politique*, but to be plausible his assessment of himself had to have some basis in fact. What, therefore, had Richelieu done in his lifetime to allow him to make the claim that he had 'tamed' the nobility? The answer, of course, is that he had put his noble influence to the service of the crown, and in order to do this he had 'tamed' certain other nobles for specific reasons. Yet it was, most definitely, not done as part of a more general royal agenda to weaken the nobility. This selective persecution in the service of the crown can be clearly illustrated with the case of a young nobleman, Montmorency-Boutteville, who was executed in 1627 at the behest of the cardinal for ignoring a recent royal ban on duelling. By executing one of the most prominent nobles in France, an example was being made of him, and a powerful statement of the king's desire to be obeyed was being announced. The application of the law in this case, however, appeared to many to be an arbitrary act of an increasingly authoritarian government.

This episode can be interpreted in a number of ways. It might seem that Louis XIII was insisting on enforcing the full extent of his authority and reminding the nobility of their subservient place. Yet this is not consistent with the rest of his reign. Louis XIII simply did not seize opportunities to chastise and humble his nobles in this way. It is, on the other hand, entirely consistent with Richelieu's actions. Thus it is hard not to sense his controlling hand. Richelieu reinforced his authority with grand gestures, but more particularly by isolating his enemies, in this case the Montmorency family. Self-evidently, the spirit of this law had been to protect the nobility from itself, to keep these important members of French society from killing each other [*Doc. 11*]. It was allowed to be used in this exceptional case in a self-serving political way, however, because Richelieu's personal political benefit also helped the immediate work of the government. Later, on a much grander scale, the head of the family, the Duke of Montmorency himself, was executed for leading a rebellion in the south of the country in 1632. Yet although such individuals or families were increasingly excluded from power, nothing indicates that, as a group, the nobility was under any threat at all during Richelieu's ministry. In his *testament politique*, Richelieu was not claiming to have emasculated the nobility as a class (an inconceivable notion at the time), nor would Louis XIII have been happy had he done so.

Richelieu was not the only noble who might be a useful servant of the crown, and although Louis XIII knew that the nobility were potentially dangerous, they were also an integral part of the body politic and could not be alienated. Thus following Richelieu's death in December 1642, a number of nobles who had been excluded during the cardinal's ministry had their political careers resurrected. It might be argued that this was permitted by Louis XIII out of fear, to satisfy demands in an attempt to avoid a noble backlash. Yet it is at least equally true that this was a perfectly natural, and from Louis XIII's perspective, pragmatic use of available political clout. Gaston d'Orléans was a high-profile example, but others such as the Duke of Vendôme also returned to the centre of the political stage. This erstwhile enemy of Richelieu returned from exile and was instrumental in the royal victory over the Fronde as the new Grand-Master of Navigation gathering ships in his former stronghold, Brittany, to repel English intervention by sea and to battle the Spanish fleet sent to protect Bordeaux during the Fronde. In the political vacuum after Richelieu's death, it would have been impossible, and indeed there would have been no advantage, to keep such people down.

Looking beyond his own death, Louis XIII prepared for the regency government of his son by formally restricting, in the terms of his will, the powers that Anne would have as regent. In doing so, he was most likely thinking back to his youth, when Concini had so thoroughly dominated the regency of his mother, Marie de Medici. To protect against this sort of factional domination during the almost inevitable noble competition for influence that would occur after his death, Louis XIII had not replaced Richelieu as such, but rather included Mazarin as part of a triumvirate of influences on an expanded inner circle within the royal council. In this way, Louis XIII was true to the principles that had defined Bourbon government since 1589. In other words, the crown worked resolutely to establish a working relationship with the nobility, as the only imaginable basis upon which to exercise practical political power, while at the same time defending the independence of the council as an expression of the royal will.

This particular arrangement, which served nobody's immediate selfish interest, did not long survive the king. Anne of Austria worked quickly in the days after her husband's death to have her full authority as regent to the young Louis XIV recognised by the parlement of Paris and Mazarin soon emerged as her favourite and the dominant voice on the council, just as Richelieu had before him. This is not specifically what Louis XIII had imagined, but the pressures of the war demanded a continuation of the most pragmatic approach to government, and Mazarin's elevation to political pre-eminence and subsequent career had been no more designed to alienate the nobility as a class than Richelieu's had been or Sully's before that.

HISTORIANS AND THE NOBILITY

One of the problems historians face when assessing the role of the nobility in French society comes from the weaknesses of the conceptual models used to describe them, including the very idea of the French nobility as a 'class'. This approach was developed in the work of a Soviet historian, Boris Porchnev, on popular rebellions prior to the Fronde. His study, first published in Russian in 1948, was largely based on exclusive access to a collection of letters held in St Petersburg which had been written to the chancellor Séguier. From these, Porchnev identified a deep-rooted tension between the peasantry and the ruling classes. The spate of popular rebellions at this time was evidence of increased class tension. Although members of the nobility, or municipal elites, occasionally lent their material and organisational support to these revolts, Porchnev argued, they were simply using popular anger and channelling it to further their interests. Inevitably, because they had so much more to lose, the privileged eventually abandoned the peasant rebels and left them to their fate. Such moments of common purpose, therefore, did not disguise for Porchnev the fact that early modern France was a society that was divided along socio-economic class lines and that there was a fundamental tension between the feudal, ruling elite and the ruled (Porchnev, 1963). Yet this idea that the poor were merely pawns, or dupes, does justice neither to the complexity of the motivations of the participants in the fields and streets of France, nor to the difficult position of the elites.

The most vociferous intellectual opponent of Porchnev was the French historian Roland Mousnier (Mousnier, 1971). He, and the many historians who have taken his lead, felt that the key lies in the traditional division of society into three estates: the clergy, the nobility and the vaguely defined 'third' estate. Within these divisions were innumerable sub-divisions, a hierarchy of 'orders' to which all people belonged. A person's identity, therefore, was not defined by wealth or class, but by one's role in society whether acquired through birth, through the purchase of public office or any other means. Thus society was not bound by horizontal ties within different classes. Rather, it was made up of different orders, or ranks (defined by current cultural ideas) which were bound vertically. That is to say that loyalty and personal affiliations were created by local concerns. An agricultural labourer in one region, for example, would have been unlikely to feel political solidarity with someone in a similar situation in a distant province. He would have been more likely to develop a sense of identity with respect to the local landlord upon whom he depended for work, the local clergyman upon whom he depended for spiritual succour and so on. Thus if an onerous tax were imposed on a region, Mousnier argued, it is no surprise if at times different groups worked together to resist. The important divisions in society were not geographical, however, but were still between these orders, for even in these moments of regional unity and harmony in a fight against the centralising forces of Paris, Mousnier suggested that each order was fighting for its own interests.

Mousnier's society of orders has been far more influential than Porchnev's model. Yet we should be wary of simply adopting the current fashion of dismissing Marxist analyses, such as Porchnev's, out of hand. Mousnier has been accused of adopting the writings of seventeenth-century political commentators uncritically and thus of simplifying and rigidly categorising people in a way that just does not do justice to the complexity of human societies or to the sheer variety of human motivations and responses. Writers such as Charles de Loyseau, who described an elaborate society of different social divisions in 1610, may not actually be the best people to judge the nature of their own society [*Doc. 7*]. One could say that they do not benefit from the objectivity provided by the passage of time. Moreover, such descriptions of different social orders tended to be written by, or for, the more privileged people in society. In other words, they may have been as much exercises in creating an ideal society, or in defending certain privileges, as in providing objective descriptions. Most historians now recognise conceptual weaknesses in both models, though they would tend to agree with Peter Burke who, if forced to choose, would accept orders over classes 'as the least misleading of the two' (Burke, 'Orders', 1992: 12).

Certainly the nobility were involved in conflict and social tensions, but these tended to occur within the nobility itself, particularly between those said to be of 'the robe' and those of 'the sword'. These labels refer to the 'new' and 'old' nobility, or those whose families had been recently ennobled through service in the expanding judiciary or administrative bureaucracy ('robe nobility' refers to the robes worn by judges or other civil servants) or the traditional nobility who owed their position to their birth within families with longstanding military obligations to the king (hence the term 'sword nobility'). Many members of the sword nobility resented the pretensions of the robe and felt that the dignity and privileges of the nobility were being undermined by these *parvenus*. This internal division has traditionally been seen as a contributory factor in the decline of the nobility as a whole and, consequently, in the rise of the absolutist state. An absolute monarch, it is said, builds a large bureaucracy which not only allows for more effective government but draws on the strengths of the ambitious, wealthy, bourgeois elements of society. As loyal servants of the crown, granted important positions and the possibility of eventual ennoblement, the bourgeoisie effectively entered into an alliance with the monarch against the increasingly anachronistic pretensions of the upper nobility. So important was this new bureaucratic 'class' to the growing power of the king that some historians refer to a 'bureaucratic monarchy' under Louis XIV rather than an absolutist one (Rule, 1969).

Although some sword nobles might have suffered in the seventeenth century, it is hard to see how they were threatened as a group, particularly by the ennoblement of people through administrative service to the crown. It should be remembered that the enormous multiplication of offices, especially in the first half of the seventeenth century, was not just due to the desperate financial straits of a government trying to find purchasers, but to a corresponding increase in demand which sent the prices soaring. This demand was not generated by people who wished to overturn the system, but rather by those who wanted to join and benefit from it. The people who invested in royal office rarely did it for financial reasons alone. More often, they entered the service of the king to better themselves and their families socially. People who sought ennoblement hoped to emulate their superiors rather than to compete with them. Indeed, it could be said that in the long view the possibility of social advancement represented by the robe nobility actually strengthened the nobility as a whole, renewing it and saving it from natural generational attrition.

Moreover, the thirst for office was not restricted to upwardly mobile bourgeois but also extended to members of what could be considered the sword nobility. This, along with intermarriage between the two groups, tends to blur the distinction. Thus without denying that there was a hierarchy within the nobility and evident social tension, the increase in numbers through office-holding did not lead to its overall decline. Instead it indicates a growing, if somewhat reluctant, acceptance of the legitimacy and social value of administrative service to the crown over the traditional definition of military obligation and birth alone.

As a consequence, historians currently tend less often to think of early modern society as shaped by deep, structural conflicts, and they put less weight on exclusive categories, or types, of noble, such as 'robe' or 'sword'. Instead there has been a concentration on personal networks of influence based on kinship, patronage and clientage. This perspective has undoubtedly improved our understanding of the nature of political power in the period, making it possible among other things to assess properly the political methods and impact of the careers of Richelieu and Mazarin. As we have seen, they developed extensive personal networks of influence, as the only way to govern effectively. Yet this was not unique to Richelieu and Mazarin. There were many interacting and overlapping networks of influence. One owed one's allegiance and political life to the patron responsible for one's success. People would unashamedly refer to themselves as political 'creatures' of others. Thus any high-ranking noble might sit atop a huge pyramid of clientage relations that reached all the way down to local village affairs. In this way, they could exercise tremendous practical authority. For example, Condé's power was based upon his birth, but also upon the offices he acquired and the clientage system he inherited and nurtured. As governor of Burgundy, in particular, his influence was so great that virtually every public office there was filled with a personal client. Though recognising the ultimate authority of the crown, Burgundians naturally saw Condé as the real, or more immediate, source of local power.

As valuable as this emphasis on clientage and kinship has been, there is a danger that as an exclusive approach to the study of the period, it might lead to over-simplification. One cannot, for example, assume equally strong bonds of loyalty in all political relationships, nor should one discount overlapping interests. An individual might feel conflicting loyalties, and the strength of the ties might constantly be in flux. It would be impossible, therefore, for an historian to delineate and accurately chart the various networks of influence. Also, an excessive concentration on clientage tends to play down the role of the monarchy. No network of noble influence was entirely independent of the crown's influence, so it could never stand on its own. More than this, it can imply that clientage networks were developed for their own sake. Clientage is useful conceptually only when it is understood that the elaboration of networks of influence was undertaken for the same purpose as virtually everything else nobles did: the improvement of the standing of their families. Dynastic interests motivated the marriages nobles entered into and negotiated for their children, where and how they chose to live and spend their money, and even who they would defend or oppose politically.

During the Fronde, nobles such as Condé were upset primarily because the cardinal-ministers were personal rivals. Despite their role as ministers to the king and cardinals of the Catholic church, it is clear from the political appointments they made, the terms of their wills and the marriages they arranged for their nieces and nephews, among other things, that Richelieu and Mazarin were as motivated by dynastic interests as any other noble (Bergin, 1985). They had been allowed to extend their network of personal clients in competition with other nobles' traditional distribution of patronage and clientage systems. From Condé's perspective, he was only fighting for the influence to which his name and his service entitled him. In short, he did not want his family marginalised or its reputation tarnished. His struggle was certainly not against growing government and royal authority in principle but to retain his family's dominant role within it. By allowing Richelieu and Mazarin to become huge power brokers and to become fabulously wealthy and influential, the crown had appealed to their dynastic interests. This made them happy, loyal and successful servants. Thus dynasticism was not just the motivating force for the Bourbon monarchs, but for their ministers of state, their nobility and indeed for the aspiring professional and merchant groups. This is the key to understanding the actions of the nobility in the seventeenth century and the resolution of the conflict between them and the monarchy by 1660.

THE DYNASTIC STATE

The reason the Fronde had become such a passionate, violent confrontation was the scale of the undertaking of the war with Spain. The crown's main ambition, to emerge successfully from this conflict, demanded an extra effort which required many compromises and sacrifices that were bound to irritate people. Yet over the course of this difficult and tumultuous century, people ultimately respected the dynastic ambitions of the king and allowed him to pursue his objectives, often at great cost to themselves, because they had similar motivations. When free to pursue these ambitions, their opposition to the monarchy collapsed. In many ways, it could be said that dynasticism is what united this society or defined its political culture. The measure of the success of the monarchy is the extent to which it used this to its advantage.

For good reason, 1661 is held up as a pivotal year in the institutional history of France. Henceforth, the king would be his own first minister, accepting direct responsibility for the affairs of state. One dissenter, James Collins, argues that the restoration of royal authority had actually begun before 1661, and the evidence was in the aftermath of the Fronde, with Louis XIV's coronation ceremony of 7 June 1654. This was an elaborate affair held, according to tradition, at the cathedral at Reims. The symbolism and ritual was designed to reinforce the sacerdotal nature of kingship and the king's contract with God. The peers of the realm and many of the great nobles were also present, formally participating in the ceremony and paying homage to the king, for Louis XIV was entering a contract with them too, along with the other people of France, to protect their interests and to rule with justice and mercy (Collins, 1995).

This was by no means the first coronation to reinforce symbolically the legal, contractual nature of monarchy, yet it was no mere empty exercise either. Louis XIV was particularly aware of the importance of ceremony, ritual and symbolism. Throughout his long reign, they would be used to re-enforce his authority and to create a veritable cult of kingship (Love, 1996). They were powerful tools in the construction of the mystique surrounding his authority, re-enforced daily by the complex etiquette and ritual of court life at the magnificent palace and gardens he would later have built in the swampy environs of his father's old hunting lodge at Versailles. Yet the nobility were not being duped into participating in a cynically contrived, elaborate stage show. All of the ceremony and grandeur associated with the reign was devised at least as much to reflect the reality of the situation as it was to reinforce and to build it. This contract between king and nobility was highly respected as was the noble commitment to an increasingly monarch-centred political culture. The person of the king, by general consensus, was indeed the focus and source of all political power.

This subtle change in the perception of the king can be detected in Louis XIV's treatment of Condé in the post-Fronde period. From his exile in the Spanish Netherlands, Condé had continued to try to foment trouble in France and had led a number of Spanish armies against his native country. He was eventually defeated by Turenne at the Battle of the Dunes on 14 June 1658. This was an important victory for Louis XIV, for it paved the way for negotiations with Spain leading to the Peace of the Pyrenees the following year. It also led to Condé's submission. In January 1660, he asked for the king's forgiveness, receiving a full pardon and the rehabilitation of his reputation.

Why did Louis XIV forgive Condé? Had this not been a chance to display his growing royal authority and reinforce his intolerance of disobedience and rebellion by arresting him and putting him on trial? No. For the king, far more important than a display of any supposed victory over the nobility was the golden opportunity to demonstrate, not just his clemency, but the solid mutual interdependence between king and noble upon which a strong monarchy must be based. As a prince of the blood and still potential heir to the throne, Condé was exceptional and for obvious dynastic reasons could not have been punished as an ordinary noble might have been. Nevertheless, his treatment at the hands of Louis XIV is indicative and consistent with that received by others in the century. As we have seen since the sixteenth-century civil wars, the reconciliation of the crown and the nobility was one of the principal priorities of government and a fundamental ambition of the monarchy.

When relations with the crown were strained during the Fronde, it was Condé's acute, and wounded, sense of his stature as a 'sword' noble which led him into revolt and then into exile. Yet Condé was able to re-establish himself after 1660 as the representation of the noble ideal by changing and adapting to the new environment in which he found himself where the king was now the undisputed source of authority and military glory. For the rest of his days, Condé was celebrated as an ideal noble, no longer for his pride and independent military strength, but for the qualities of good taste, refinement and obedience to the king (Bannister, 2000). He spent his time cultivating his lifestyle at his chateau at Chantilly and promoting this role in high society. In this way, he embodied a cultural shift away from the values of the independent noble warrior towards those of the courtier gentleman. Noble behaviour had become less violent and more refined in the course of the seventeenth century, not because the nobles had been emasculated by an avaricious monarchy but because they had been allowed to retain a pre-eminent place in society in this way.

More importantly, perhaps, Condé readily accepted his new role in part because it did not challenge his status, as a traditional sword noble, over the lower nobility. The quality of birth remained an essential defining qualification for nobility. Much of Louis XIV's success was in recognising the importance of this idea and of retaining for the high nobility a military role which could satisfy their dynastic ambitions. As recent work by Guy Rowlands reveals, although there were many changes in the organisation of the army over the course of the seventeenth century, including an undeniable authoritarian approach by the crown, the nobility did not lose their privileged place. Even within an expanded, more professional army, they continued to hold many of the key military commands. Their military reputations, therefore, would no longer be won at the head of semi-private regiments but in the king's name, for he insisted on a monopoly on military glory. So although there would no longer be a place in French society for independent military action by nobles, there was nevertheless still an opportunity to build a military reputation and to reinforce the status of their exulted lineage.

Over the course of the first sixty years of the seventeenth century, the French crown stretched its relations with its subjects almost to breaking point. It survived, indeed it thrived by 1661, not because of an ambition to centralise authority in royal hands or in those of a powerful principal minister, nor was it simply because of an enlarged or somewhat more modernised bureaucracy and tax-raising machinery. Whatever can be said about the efficiency or effectiveness of the increased scale of government, it reflects greater consensus in government and the desire to participate in it. In this light, the increased bureaucratic control is less a cause than a reflection of the crown's success. With the same demographic and tax base as Louis XIII had, Louis XIV was able to gather far larger armies and to support them permanently in the decades after 1661. He was able to do this largely because of his sensitivity to the dynastic interests of his leading subjects. He was able to respect them, reward them and play them off to his advantage. His appointments to the high command within his greatly expanded army, for example, were made very carefully, satisfying the dynastic interests of his leading nobles without ever becoming beholden to them. This was not just a clever ploy, or an important departure, but a natural response by a monarch unlikely to have been able to imagine a state based on anything other than noble interest. This is not to play down the personal role of Louis XIV or others in the recovery of royal authority, for it is the success of the crown and of the government in the pursuit of its longstanding aims, and in particular that over the Fronde, that provided the king with a particularly favourable climate to give full expression to his political instincts. These dynastic instincts were shared, not only by leading nobles, but by virtually all elements of French society at the time, and they lie at the heart of the success of Louis XIV's subsequent reign and the fashioning of what Rowlands describes as the 'dynastic state' (Rowlands, 2002).

PART THREE ASSESSMENT

CHAPTER SIX

THE ORIGINS OF FRENCH ABSOLUTISM?

In 1652 the crown was at war with its own subjects; the capital city was in chaos and there was widespread devastation in the surrounding countryside. Less than ten years later, one of the most celebrated periods of French history dawned with the 'personal' rule of Louis XIV. Though not without its critics, its setbacks and suffering, this reign to 1715 was certainly long and glorious and traditionally held by historians as the apotheosis of royal absolutism. We would do well, therefore, to reflect upon these crucial years up to 1661 and consider just how the monarchy was able to reposition itself in such apparently dramatic fashion. What happened in these nine years? Had Louis XIV been traumatised by the Fronde, growing up with a new-found determination never again to allow divisions and disobedience to disrupt his realm? Had the government under the restored Cardinal Mazarin managed to strengthen the pillars of the monarchy to such an extent that it could now rule without any opposition or hindrance?

It is certainly true that the king displayed growing authoritarian tendencies and that he matched his words with actions. Yet there is a temptation for historians to exaggerate the strength of the monarchy in the years after the end of the Fronde from 1653. The rebels had been defeated, but on its own this did little to alleviate the difficulties the government faced. It should not be forgotten that France was still mired in a protracted, difficult war. Vocal opposition continued to ring in Paris, especially on religious matters, and in the country at large violent rebellions continued to erupt. Certainly these were momentous years. Yet what was remarkable was not how Mazarin positioned France for future greatness, but how thoroughly, and suddenly, existing, long-standing ambitions were met.

In three climactic years, between 1659 and 1661, Louis XIV was in a position to insist on doctrinal purity and obedience in spiritual matters, to bring a successful end to the war with Spain in the process securing the reputation and future of his dynasty, and to reconcile the nobility. It could be said, then, that the crown had satisfied every fundamental ambition it had held for centuries. Yet to understand these three years a distinction between 'strength' and 'success' must be drawn. Facing all of the same challenges and dangers, Mazarin's still fragile ministry conducted itself in familiar fashion, and it did so in the pursuit of traditional aims. If anything can be said to have emerged from the decade after 1653, it is simply the effect of this remarkable sequence of events. It can certainly account for the uncommon enthusiasm and vigour with which Louis XIV embarked on his personal reign [*Doc. 39*]. More importantly, along with this success came a wider consensus within France, a greater willingness to embrace the revitalised monarchy. As much as anything else, this was the origin of the style of government which has come to be known as absolutism. Although it is possible to identify a trends towards greater centralisation and royal authority throughout the century, the monarchy was not on a set path of development. In 1661, it remained to be seen what opportunities would be opened and pursued, that is to say just what effect this success would have in practice.

THE FOUQUET-COLBERT RIVALRY

The test of the effectiveness of any early-modern government is its ability to raise money and collect taxes. The crown had won a comprehensive military and political victory in the Fronde, though it faced a financial challenge every bit as serious as ever. Indeed the crown's finances had been severely disrupted, so its revenues were mortgaged many years into the future. Though most of the obnoxious legislative obstacles erected by the Fronde were now removed, the government was still left with an unpopular, expensive war, a clumsy inefficient bureaucracy and the services of a number of hated tax farmers. Moreover, its credit was at an impossibly low point among potential money lenders. This would be a serious test of the crown's ability to extract and manipulate the resources of the kingdom. That Mazarin died in office, the richest subject in the history of France to date, having brought the war to a satisfactory conclusion, is a remarkable accomplishment and actually a vindication of sorts of the often-derided fiscal practices and expedients that had for so long served the Bourbon kings. Critics could remark that the fiscal operations of the government were not properly reformed after the Fronde. Yet serious reform was never even attempted, nor indeed is it obvious that it would have brought better results.

The key to the survival of the government in these years of dire financial straits were the political wiles and machinations within the world of the financiers of Mazarin and of Nicolas Fouquet, the son of a client of Richelieu, who was a superintendent of finance from 1653 to 1661. Mazarin's personal fortune, which had collapsed during the Fronde, skyrocketed thereafter, not just a sign of his personal avarice but a positive confirmation of the interconnection between public and private finances upon which the crown relied. Mazarin, it seems, became the embodiment of the king's finances, operating not according to any bureaucratic plan, or even within any meaningful legal boundaries, but on a hand-to-mouth basis. Thus as he became wealthy like no other French subject had before, he managed to keep the system operating.

Under Mazarin and Fouquet, royal expenditure and taxation both increased, and provincial *intendants* were reintroduced to help with financial administration. Significantly, investigations by the parlements into the affairs of many financiers were stopped and, partly as a result, after 1655 government borrowing increased dramatically. By the late 1650s, Mazarin and Fouquet had arguably become greater political and financial patrons and power brokers than the king himself, and though this may have provided political fodder for their detractors, it had actually also served the ambitions of the king very well. If the victory over the Fronde had indeed opened a window of opportunity for the crown to impose far-reaching administrative reforms to put the royal finances on a sound footing for the future and to stamp out corruption and secret dealings, that opportunity was declined.

The success of Mazarin's ministry is often overshadowed in historical accounts by the advent of Jean-Baptiste Colbert and the financial initiatives he undertook as one of Louis XIV's most trusted councillors after 1661. Colbert, whose methods were more open and recognisably modern, is often presented in a more favourable light. Nevertheless, in a familiar pattern, he owed his early career and position of influence to a sustained political attack against his rival, Fouquet. The determination with which Colbert engineered the downfall and arrest of Fouquet, who was also condemned in the harshest terms by Louis XIV, however, is less evidence of a new departure in financial administration than of personal rivalry. Colbert's merits as an administrator and his later accomplishments notwithstanding, Fouquet had been a casualty of an aggressive political campaign.

According to traditional accounts of the reign of Louis XIV, in August 1661 Nicolas Fouquet hosted a lavish party at his exquisite new palace at Vaux-le-Vicomte. So grand was the affair that the king became jealous of his influence and his ambition and had him arrested and imprisoned for life. He then eliminated the post of superintendent of finance and replaced it with a more accountable 'royal council of finance' as part of the construction of a new-style monarchy. To some extent, therefore, Fouquet's arrest and exile marks a new departure. Out of chaos, disorder and peculation came accountability, transparency and modernisation.

Nobody better embodies this new spirit of government, it is argued, than Colbert. Although he could not aspire to the now defunct position of principal minister after 1661, Colbert had enormous influence in his multiple roles as secretary of state for the royal household, Paris, the clergy and the navy, superintendent of public works and controller-general of finance. In this last capacity, he is credited with bringing the royal finances under control and with leading something of a financial miracle. He was the driving force behind the codification and regularisation of the country's many laws. And, he was responsible for many ambitious plans for commercial expansion on a grand scale. In many ways, therefore, he is the perfect complement to the king's ambitions and an icon of the new age: a forward-thinking, modern bureaucrat who was entirely loyal to the king, working in his interests alone.

The work of Daniel Dessert, however, has levelled a serious blow to the reputation of Colbert while resurrecting that of Fouquet. By implication, Dessert plays down the significance of the transition from Fouquet to Colbert in 1661. He suggests that despite the appearance of significant change, Colbert operated in much the same way that Fouquet had (Dessert, 1987). The network of Fouquet's relations and clients which had come to dominate financial and political circles was simply replaced by another, 'la filiale Colbert' (Dessert, 1995). That is to say that Colbert simply purged Fouquet's relations and replaced them with his own. Far from being modern, impartial and bureaucratic, therefore, the government of Louis XIV continued to operate through personal political connections and influence within the murky world of the financiers. Though he would never be in a position to match the enormous fortunes of the cardinal-ministers, nor indeed even the estimated worth of Fouquet of 15.4 million *livres* in 1661, Colbert still managed to acquire a sizeable fortune of nearly 6 million over his twenty two years in office.

The green light for Colbert to conspire earnestly against his target had come in 1659 with the death of Abel Servien, who had been co-superintendent of finance with Fouquet since 1653. Fouquet was then accused of all manner of financial irregularity. To the charge that he had been extravagant and built a sizeable fortune, Fouquet was willing to admit. As for the rest, he claimed he had done nothing unusual. He was charged with borrowing money on behalf of the crown unnecessarily and with illegally lending money to the king himself and profiting from it. He was also accused of a litany of other abuses, including taking illicit payments from contractors and participating in tax farms under assumed names.

Although he denied many of these charges, it seems that Fouquet's defence was based less on denial than the argument that there was nothing new or illegal about these practices. Indeed, this tells us much about the conduct of affairs under Mazarin who he claimed actually had had no real system, effectively managing the finances of the kingdom by channelling them through his own hands and giving orders to Fouquet almost willy-nilly. Fouquet's principal defence, that although he lent money to the king he was only following Mazarin's verbal orders, would be impossible to prove. If he is to be believed, he offered loans to the crown at lower rates of interest than usual and at a time when other lenders were proving reluctant. Nevertheless, it is fair to say that Fouquet had been left to do the best he could in a time of crisis with an inadequate tax system. From Dessert's perspective, therefore,

Fouquet did a commendable job of keeping the royal finances afloat, and his defence in court is said to have been so compelling that some of the prosecutors were embarrassed to press their case.

Colbert, who was instrumental in the convocation of a *chambre de justice* against Fouquet, had the most to gain from his downfall. It is less immediately obvious why Louis XIV allowed him to become the object of a distasteful and vicious political witch-hunt, and indeed why his preferred punishment for Fouquet was execution. It is far-fetched to suggest that he was appalled by Fouquet's financial methods, for not only had they been successful and helped the crown weather a difficult storm, as he claimed, they were consistent with those of his predecessors, and indeed of the king's own principal minister. This last is a key point and probably accounts for the king's determination. Had Fouquet simply been removed from office to make way for a preferred candidate in Colbert, he would not only have insisted on the twelve million *livres* he claimed was owed to him from outstanding loans to the crown, he would have deflected criticism towards his former political master, Mazarin. Louis XIV needed to protect the reputation of the man to whom he had been so personally indebted and in whom he had placed so much political trust. In this sense, the king's vehement renunciation of Fouquet was a measure of Mazarin's success as a minister. Colbert, too, had reason to avoid a protracted investigation or public debate on ethical grounds with Fouquet, for he was just as implicated in Mazarin's financial dealings as Fouquet had been. Colbert had risen through the ranks in Mazarin's service as his *intendant de la maison*. In other words, he had been largely responsible for the very rapid creation of the greatest personal fortune in the history of the realm of between 35 and 37 million *livres*. If anything untoward about Mazarin and the fiscal dealings of his ministry was to be revealed, then Colbert was an accessory with a great deal to hide. Thus if Fouquet had to fall, and his many clients with him, to make way for Colbert, then he had to fall hard and fast. This was a political attack, not a positive reform of what had, after all, been a largely successful financial career.

THE END OF GOVERNMENT BY FIRST MINISTER?

It has been argued that in not being able to foresee his downfall Fouquet displayed political naiveté. Richard Bonney suggests that he did not fit in with a new 'ethic' of accountability and financial regularity in government that was developing along with a growing distinction between public and private finance. Colbert outmanoeuvred him in forging a 'common purpose' with the king by helping to construct the image which Louis XIV wanted to convey of himself. A successful servant would henceforth always have to appear, at least, to be putting the king's interests before his own, for Louis XIV was determined to be in control of affairs of state. Moreover, the sheer scale of government now simply demanded more regular and open financial administration. The relatively modest fortune accumulated by Colbert compared with that of the previous ministers reinforces Bonney's claim that the opportunities for peculation and self-aggrandisement simply were no longer available in the new political environment (Bonney, 1996).

This is an extremely valuable perspective, though in many ways the persecution of Fouquet or the elimination of the role of first minister after Mazarin's death was not a new departure. Louis XIV had inherited a distaste for factional domination of government at the highest level from his predecessors, and in Fouquet he saw a familiar danger, for it seems that Fouquet simply assumed that he would be the natural successor to Mazarin. To be fair, Fouquet had been a loyal servant of Mazarin; he had the track-record and experience, the stature and crucially the wealth to fill the role effectively. The king's implacable opposition, however, was not due to a new-found, principled determination never to allow an individual minister of state to dominate the country's financial affairs. This was not a bold, conscious rejection of government by first minister in principle. It was, in fact, entirely consistent with the decision-making of the two previous Bourbon monarchs who both actively sought to protect the integrity of the royal council.

As we have seen, there had been a series of principal ministers since Sully's elevation to political pre-eminence by 1605. Yet none of these ministers had risen to their positions as a matter of course. This was not simply an office to which one could graduate or which one could earn; it was, rather more nebulously, a position of trust for which one had to be chosen by the king, for the very purpose of privileging ministers in this way had been to guarantee an independent royal authority in the council and to guard against the potentially pernicious influence of other nobles. In other words, there had never been government by first minister as an ideal type. These men had, in fact, been a part of an emerging process that the 1661 settlement embodied by which the king maintained his pre-eminence against other powerful figures. The closest parallel to Fouquet's arrogance had been that of Concini, who had also assumed a dominant place on the regency council of Marie de Medici. As a reward for his ambition, he met an even worse fate than Fouquet when he was murdered on the orders of Louis XIII within months of the latter attaining his majority! As for Louis XIV, although not opposed in principle or in practice to Fouquet's wealth, political methods or financial dealings, he would simply not have been able to tolerate a natural succession to the position of first minister and the implied lack of control of his council.

Louis XIV's actions echoed those of his father in other ways too. As Richard Bonney has pointed out, in December 1621 when Luynes died Louis XIII announced his decision to rule personally (Bonney, 1991: 227). In this case, he was neither denying the advantages hitherto enjoyed from, nor closing the door to future close collaboration with, a powerful minister. He was, in fact, simply confirming the supremacy of his position. Equally, Louis XIII's decision to establish a regency council after Richelieu's death in 1642 with a triumvirate of powerful voices has echoes in that later taken by Louis XIV to replace Mazarin with a council dominated by loyal servants through the years of the Fronde: Lionne, Le Tellier and initially Fouquet (later replaced by Colbert, of course). Though not taken from the same position of weakness, this decision by Louis XIV was similar in that, in the absence of a strong royal card in the guise of a suitable principal minister, a balance of influence on the council was seen as probably the best protection against factional dominance.

Without denying the strength of Louis XIV's personality and his eagerness to assume greater responsibility for governing, or the increasing scale of government which alone required a larger, more efficient and structured bureaucracy, the decisions taken in 1661 display less innovation than consistency with long-standing tendencies in government. Patronage, clientage and personal influence would remain the keys to successful government. Yet more than ever, this influence would be seen to be emanating exclusively and directly from the king. There was no longer obvious, potentially divisive intermediaries such as the cardinal-ministers, and now with the active, guiding hand of the adult king, the reformed council was more likely to succeed. It would now be much easier to manage the personal ambitions of the nobility, and of everyone else for that matter, if they were all looking to the king for favour. In this respect, Louis XIV himself deserves a lot of credit for the changes that followed. It was undoubtedly a necessary precondition for the continued growth of the state and of France's stature as a great power. For a broad political consensus to emerge, which is necessary for a strong government, power had to be seen to be coming from the king, not from a faction that might happen to have muscled its way to power. Again, however, this was not a new principle, and it did not preclude the methods, nor the uncommon influence, of ministers such as Richelieu and Mazarin in the future. Louis XIV himself had, after all, supported and protected Mazarin in very difficult times. Indeed, if anything symbolises the post-Fronde period of government, it is the continued political pre-eminence of Cardinal Mazarin. Louis XIV seems to have been determined to defy popular demands and very purposefully to reinstate and protect Mazarin, the focus of so much *frondeur* fury, as a statement of his own authority. Rather than seeing the demise of government by first minister in 1661, we could just as easily see its perfection, for the position was not so much eliminated by Louis XIV as filled by him.

THE GOLDEN YEARS, 1659–61

Thus it could be said that in arresting Fouquet and embarking on his 'personal' reign in 1661, Louis XIV was actually vindicating existing political and fiscal practices. Yet even more remarkable than any continuity in method in this period is the extent to which the fundamental spiritual, military and dynastic ambitions of the monarchy were met at the same time. At times this success was dramatic, as with Louis XIV's unequivocal treatment of the city of Marseille.

Marseille was a very old city which, while recognising the formal authority of the crown, was in many practical respects independent, enjoying a number of fiscal privileges. Since the sixteenth century when it had been temporarily governed by the Catholic League in opposition to Henri IV's claim to the throne, Marseille had always been a headache. By embracing the Fronde, it merely confirmed its troublesome reputation. Taking the opportunity that peace with Spain offered in 1659, Louis XIV responded with force to an uprising against a client of Mazarin in the area, the president of the parlement at Aix. With a telling lack of subtlety, he arrived with an army of 6,000 men in January 1660 and demanded the city's submission. When the doors were finally opened, the king refused to enter through them, choosing instead a breach that had opened in the walls. The message was clear. Louis XIV had conquered Marseille; he had not negotiated with it. As a result, his will would prevail. At a stroke, Marseille's centuries-old constitution was swept aside. The structure of the municipal government was changed to guarantee obedience to royal authority, and part of the city's defences were pulled down and reconstructed. This episode could well stand as a symbol of a new age of French government in which the crown would rule with an iron fist. Yet it is also reminiscent of Louis XIII's campaign to Béarn in 1620 to impose Catholic worship in the area. Neither was imposing his will simply to acquire power, nor interfering with municipal immunities for its own sake, but responding to what they saw as acts of open disobedience with an appropriate show of force.

If we compare these actions with those at La Rochelle in 1627–28 and Bordeaux in 1652–53, as two of the most notable incidents of armed repression of municipal governments, we can see a pattern of behaviour. Both of these cities were also seen by the crown as potentially troublesome, each with a long history of relative constitutional autonomy and fiscal privileges which they protected fiercely. Moreover, both had active maritime economies and overseas links to other powers potentially hostile to France. In 1614, a group of 'radicals' who felt excluded from local power staged a coup at La Rochelle, leading eventually to armed conflict with the crown under the direction of a small group of disaffected nobles; the same happened in Bordeaux. In one case, however, it was the continuing age of religious conflict which provided the emotive force for fullscale rebellion and for the corresponding earnestness with which the crown responded. In the other, it was the language of political defiance of the Fronde. The Bourbon monarchy had been consistently willing, and able, to reply with force, not automatically, but when its dignity was affronted. Arguably, Louis XIV's intervention in Marseille was more decisive and effective, even though there was less at stake. Nevertheless, there was nothing arbitrary or ground-breaking about it.

Less dramatically, but probably more significantly, Louis XIV demanded conformity and obedience from the Jansenists in 1660. By only tolerating a piety which recognised his role as the secular expression of God's authority, he was fulfilling perhaps the greatest ambition of his grandfather, Henri IV. Guaranteeing religious conformity was not only the duty of monarchs, if successful it was the surest means of stabilising and consolidating their authority. Naturally, Louis XIV did not actually eliminate religious discord with the stroke of a pen, but he was successfully claiming and exercising an undisputed right to impose a religious settlement. Whatever assessment one might make of the wisdom of the revocation of the Edict of Nantes in 1685, Louis XIV was exercising a spiritual authority that would have been unrecognisable to Henri IV, the author of that tortuous compromise of 1598.

Equally, when the prince of Condé pleaded for forgiveness in 1660 for his rebellious past, he showed that even the most recalcitrant noble could accept that his interests lay within a political system which was centred increasingly upon the king himself. At the same time, Louis XIV demonstrated his willingness, indeed his need, to embrace the nobility, to respect their status and their dynastic ambitions. Not only had the elusive goal of a manageable, peaceful partnership between the crown and the nobility been achieved, but the return of Condé from Spanish service also reinforced Louis XIV's victory in 1659 over France's traditional foe and its greatest international threat since the Italian wars of the early sixteenth century. The marriages arranged to secure this peace were invaluable to Louis XIV's dynastic ambitions leading indirectly to a Bourbon on the Spanish throne in the eighteenth century. With the birth of a son and potential heir in 1661 as fulfilment of the most important and basic of dynastic needs, virtually everything the Bourbon monarchy had ever aspired to seemed to be at least momentarily satisfied.

Though by no means above reproach or criticism, the government had largely met the not inconsiderable demands placed on it. Its methods, one must conclude, were sensible and appropriate, for they had allowed the crown to achieve all that it had set out to achieve. Experiments with the fundamental reform of government, which to modern observers seem like logical, self-evidently desirable means of modernisation, or the commercial invigoration and expansion of the role of the state, were not entirely ignored. Many proposals were considered, even solicited, but they were treated only as possible *desiderata*, always ancillary to the main priorities, which were defined more by the interests of the king than by what we might call today the interests of the state. It is impossible to believe that the so-called architects of the absolutist state, Sully, Richelieu or Mazarin, had ever dreamt of anything more than what was achieved in this remarkable convergence of successes between 1659 and 1661.

CONCLUSION

Much work has been done in recent decades to dispel the myth of a slowly, but inexorably, rising absolutist state that could no longer tolerate dissent. It has become abundantly clear that the theoretically unlimited right of the crown to impose its will was actually severely circumscribed by: formal bodies, such as the parlements or the estates of the kingdom; a still very powerful nobility; the financial and administrative inadequacies of a government apparatus unprepared for the challenges of the seventeenth century; and the practical considerations involved in ruling such a vast country with entrenched regional identities and legal traditions in a pre-industrial age. The perspective all of this work affords has undoubtedly improved immeasurably our understanding of the function of early modern government. Yet, somewhat ironically, a continued effort to delineate the 'limits' of absolutism suffers from a similar conceptual weakness as that of nineteenth-century French national historians who sought to celebrate the achievements of the great state-builders of their past. To a certain extent, such an approach still takes as read an absolutist agenda by the monarchy and its government, albeit an unspoken and largely unsuccessful one.

Some now believe, on the one hand, that the government struggled over the course of the century against very real constraints to its effective authority, though its will ultimately prevailed and its authority was reinforced in the process. Others stress the strength of these constraints and feel that the compromises the crown constantly had to make meant that it was effectively beholden to its subjects, or at least its most powerful ones, and therefore had to rule in consultation with them, or the institutions of government said to represent their interests. Yet whether one chooses to credit the crown's authority or the continuing political influence, in various forms, of its subjects, a certain conscious desire on the part of the crown to increase its authority and to eliminate opposition is still implied. Neither the crown nor its ministers, however, harboured a plan to create a centralised, bureaucratic or 'absolutist' state designed with the purpose of leading more modern, efficient armies or rationalising the process of government. This is an anachronistic assessment that could only ever have been applied retrospectively to the changes that were effected in the course of the government's dealings with its subjects. The growth in the size of government that resulted from France's foreign wars inevitably brought changes in the structure, organisation and even in some of the principles of government, some of which strengthened the effective authority of the crown. Yet this is not evidence of a plan to create a new, more powerful system of government, except inasmuch as all politicians exploit opportunities for personal advantage, and all governments do what they can to ensure their own survival.

The debate about whether the crown was 'absolutist' or 'consultative' largely misses the point. The heavy emphasis placed by historians on the extent and nature of monarchical authority, and on the origins and growth of the modern state in the seventeenth century, tends to obscure the purpose of government. It is on this basis alone that an assessment of the government's record should be made, not its incidental institutional legacy. In some studies, the emphasis on the lack of positive reform, the mismanagement of the state finances and the unimaginative direction of the armed forces, almost seems to suggest that any French success was due only to good fortune and to Spain's relative weakness. From this perspective, the traditional historical orthodoxy of rising absolutism has been revised so thoroughly that it seems France survived in spite of the efforts of Richelieu and Mazarin, not because of them. Clearly, however, France's fortunes were not determined simply by chance. Nor indeed was its success a function of the strength or weakness of its institutions of government or its bureaucracy alone. Rather, as much recent work implies, including that on the personal and political careers of Richelieu and Mazarin, royal interests depended upon the manipulation of personal relationships of power, and in the cardinal-ministers the crown found excellent servants.

Historians may choose to see royal authority as severely limited in this way, but to the kings and their ministers this was the normal state of affairs. What are often seen by historians as restrictions simply defined the boundaries within which people operated. From this point of view, the years 1598 to 1661 were good ones for France. The methods employed to keep the creaky financial machinery of state operating and to secure the necessary political stability might not have modernised the state to the extent once believed. They may even be the source of the long-term weakness of the French monarchy, but they made possible the remarkable concatenation of realised ambitions, when everything the Bourbon monarchy had striven for was achieved. David Sturdy is quite correct, therefore, to say that there was no 'ministerial' or 'bureaucratic' revolution in place. Yet neither were Richelieu and Mazarin determined constitutional guardians for whom 'the principal aim was to restore royal authority to the point at which the king could rule alone' (Sturdy, 2004:151). Their principal aim was, in fact, to survive and prosper by serving the existing personal ambitions of their king, an aim which did not necessarily require or preclude progress and innovation in government.

All of the following translations, apart from number seven, are the author's own.

HENRI IV TO THE BISHOP OF RENNES, 7 MARCH 1598

This letter from the king, prior to the promulgation of the Edict of Nantes and the Peace of Vervins, explains his confessional and military strategy . . .

I have before me an enemy [Spain] who is such a challenge as to occupy all of my energy . . . I know he still does all he can to spark a new fire in my kingdom through the Catholics who are fighting those of the Religion [the Huguenots].

If I am forced to concede more to the Huguenots than in the edict of 1577, may His Holiness [the Pope] believe that I do it to avoid an even greater evil and to favour and fortify the Catholic religion all the more, that I will do it to please and to reassure the majority of those of the said Religion [the Huguenots], and in so doing, more easily overturn the designs of the ambitious and factious among them who do what they can to drive to despair the others under my protection and to cause friction with the Catholics, who still live in large numbers in the cities that they occupy and whence they would have been forced to flee had I not intervened.

Nothing preserves the authority of princes like reputation, especially in this kingdom, based upon a nobility whose profession is honour and who sacrifice their blood to acquire it.

My sword and my faith in my allies, second only to the grace and bounty of God, is what secured the crown on my head, which had been tottering through the corruptions and seductions of my enemies. The one and the other must maintain and guarantee it, and may I lose my life rather than finish the war otherwise than with the honour with which I began it and have since executed it. The rumour of peace talks is very damaging to me because my enemies are claiming that I am behind it in order to undermine me . . .

Beger de Xivrey (ed.) (1848) *Les Lettres missives de Henri IV*, vol. 4. Paris: Imprimerie Nationale, pp. 921–2.

HENRI IV TO THE CONSTABLE, HENRY OF MONTMORENCY, 5 APRIL 1598

This letter from the king, about one week before the promulgation of the Edict of Nantes, suggests that his immediate priorities lay with forcing the submission of the rebellious Duke of Mercoeur, the governor of Brittany who was allied with Spain, and with taking remaining towns and defeating lingering Spanish forces there, especially in the Breton port of Blavet, and also in Picardy.

[A]fter the edict in favour of my cousin the Duke of Mercoeur was verified in the parlements, I sent my cousin, the Duke of Retz, to Nantes to take the city and the fortress from the soldiers that Mercoeur had left there and to establish the garrison that I ordered . . . I am leaving the day after tomorrow and will arrive at Nantes on Friday or Saturday where I will stay for only five or six days to take care of some general business for the province and whatever is necessary for the siege of Blavet where I have sent my cousin the Marshal of Brissac with Breton forces and some regiments from my army having ordered the others to return to Picardy, where I hope to go shortly, not wishing to remain in Brittany any longer than is necessary for me to get to Rennes and to give the orders required for the said siege of Blavet, out of the desire I have to get to the frontier of Picardy to make war against my enemies or, by my presence, make the conditions for a peace treaty more advantageous. In the meantime, I pray you continue to guarantee the security of the frontier and inform me frequently of any developments . . .

Beger de Xivrey (ed.) (1848) *Les Lettres missives de Henri IV*,
vol. 4. Paris: Imprimerie Nationale, p. 948.

DOCUMENT 3   **HENRI IV ON THE PROMULGATION OF THE EDICT OF NANTES, 5 MAY 1598**

In this brief note to a correspondent close to the king, Henri IV makes a reference, very rare in 1598, to the religious settlement in the Edict of Nantes.

This note . . . is to ask you to send me immediately a dozen salted geese from Béarn, the fattest that you can find, of the sort that will do the area proud. For as for my news, I can tell you that having brought this province to obedience, as soon as I have made a tour to Rennes, Dinan, and St Malo, where I am headed, I will return to the frontier with Picardy, hoping to get to Paris by the end of the month. I have brought an end to the matter with those of the Religion [the Huguenots], and on this my mind is at ease . . .

Beger de Xivrey (ed.) (1848) *Les Lettres missives de Henri IV*,
vol. 4. Paris: Imprimerie Nationale, p. 981.

DOCUMENT 4   **SULLY ON OPPOSITION TO THE ARTICLE OF THE EDICT OF NANTES RELATING TO SYNODAL ASSEMBLIES, 1599**

As soon as the Edict of Nantes was presented to the courts for registration, Henri IV faced considerable opposition. Here, Sully reflects on one of the most objectionable elements from the point of view of many Catholics.

[T]he sovereign courts . . . as much from their own initiative as at the instigation of the deputies of the Assembly of the Clergy of France who found themselves still in session, the rector of the University, the Sorbonne, and other zealous Catholics, had enormous difficulty with many of the articles . . . as all the above opponents saw that . . . it was permitted to those of the Religion to hold whatever assemblies in whichever place, wherever and however often as they pleased without asking for permission from the king or from his magistrates . . . [and] the parlement came to make great complaints to the king, remonstrating that in this way his royal authority was greatly injured, his magistrates scorned, the kingdom denied its ancient rights, and freedom [was] given to his subjects to go and intrigue and conduct underhanded practices outside of France as they like and to foreigners to do the same within France . . .

David Buisseret and Bernard Barbiche (eds) (1988) Les oeconomies royales de Sully,
vol. II, 1595–1599. Paris: Soc. de l'hist. de France, pp. 341–2.

| DOCUMENT 5 | OPPOSITION TO THE ESTABLISHMENT OF CATHOLICISM IN BÉARN, JULY 1599 |

Henri IV expresses his determination to re-establish Catholicism in his native Béarn in a letter to an officer.

. . . [Y]ou have done me a good service by advising that you predict that some are planning to remonstrate against the registration of my edict re-establishing the Catholic religion in my country of Béarn, but this notwithstanding I do not wish its verification to be deferred. For this, you are to carry yourself in this affair with such resolve that I am obeyed. You cannot know how important this is for me at present, including at Rome where this would help with my affairs there, of which you can well judge the importance . . .

J. Nouaillac (ed.) (1913) Henri IV: Raconté par lui-même.
Choix de lettres . . . Paris: Picard, pp. 293–4.

| DOCUMENT 6 | HENRI IV TO SULLY, 17 MARCH 1606 |

A letter from the king reflecting on the rebellion of the Duke of Bouillon.

My friend, it seems from the murmurings of the friends of the Duke of Bouillon that they believe that we are lacking in courage or the means to bring them around by force of arms . . . But I hope soon to disabuse them of this opinion, which is why I pray you to hurry with all that is necessary. And I will tell you that this evening I have begun to get over this terrible cold so that I think that I shall soon be free of it. I nearly got a stag today, but yesterday

I got two wolves which I take as an omen that I will be overcoming all of the miserable beasts who will oppose my will . . .

J. Nouaillac (ed.) (1913) *Henri IV: Raconté par lui-même. Choix de lettres* . . . Paris: Picard, pp. 340–1.

DOCUMENT 7   CHARLES DE LOYSEAU ON 'THE HIGH NOBILITY', 1610

From Charles de Loyseau's reflections on the structure of French society and the 'orders' by which it is made.

Although in France certain fiefs are called noble, they are not called such 'by effect, but rather by particular quality'. That is to say, it is not because they have the power to ennoble their possessor, but because of their proper dignity they are assigned to persons already noble, and cannot be held by commoners. It would indeed be contrary to reason that a commoner should be lord of a fief of dignity which carries knighthood and high nobility. So a commoner invested by someone other than the king himself can be sued either by the king's proctor, or by his feudal lord (albeit other than the one who invested him), or his heir, and even by vassals of the fief, to surrender it to a capable person. Thus, following the law, things are related to persons, and not persons to things.

As it is repugnant that the possessor of a fief of dignity should be a commoner, there are some apparent grounds for holding that those who possess these fiefs are presumed noble. To that extent they are in possession of high nobility. Therefore, if the father and the grandfather have possessed such fiefs consecutively, nobility thenceforth is prescribed for their descendants.

Translated by Howell A. Lloyd. Howell A. Lloyd (ed.) (1994) *A Treatise of Orders and Plain Dignities*. Cambridge: Cambridge University Press, pp. 135–6.

DOCUMENT 8   THE PRINCE OF CONDÉ TO DUPLESSIS-MORNAY, FEBRUARY 1614

In this letter to the influential Huguenot leader and writer, Henri de Bourbon, Prince of Condé, attempts to rally opposition to the regency government of Marie de Medici.

Sir . . . I send you this messenger expressly to keep you abreast of developments and of the just reasons which have moved us to complain of the poor management of government. I hope that, recognising the Spanish faction prevailing at court, and arms being taken up, this will serve as a serious warning that the aim is to oppress the royal household and, particularly, those of the religion of whom you are among the greatest and most important. Help me, therefore, to make known the common interest which those of the religion have with this worthy campaign, and particularly help us through your assistance. This is the service of the king, the aim of all great men, and the fulfilment of your purpose. Do not suffer oppression, and trust that we are so minded that, desirous of peace and an end to the disorders through humble remonstrance, we nevertheless do not fear war . . .

Treuttel and Würtz (eds) (1825) *Mémoires et correspondance de Duplessis-Mornay*,
vol. 12. Paris: Crapelet, p. 521.

DOCUMENT 9   **RICHELIEU'S THOUGHTS ON THE MOST PRESSING NEEDS OF FRANCE, 1624**

The two clearest indicators from which one can predict the decline of this state are seeing royal authority neglected, weak, and fallen, which leads most of the subjects, in contempt of the commands of their prince, to throw themselves into any manner of cabal to the great prejudice of the service of the king and the peace of the kingdom.

The other is excessive luxury, either in clothes, at the table, or in furnishings which has risen today to such a degree that one can no longer see the difference, from their clothes, between the prince and the gentleman, the noble from the commoner, nor the master from the servant, the manner of living of the one and the other on a par with that of the princes such that, not being able to afford their excessive expenses, most of them go to ruin or engage in crime and violence and other such immoral things . . . [I]t is essential, as soon as possible, to find the money to maintain an army in order to keep the kingdom armed with sufficient forces to defend it from abroad and to keep the subjects in their place within . . .

With these two concerns met, the king will find himself much stronger, for the great expenses into which the vanity of these days throws people and from which follows the ruin of many families, especially of the nobility, has caused much hardship and forced them to bother His Majesty continually for redress . . .

One of the principal maxims that the king must follow is to keep his court as small as he can so that His Majesty will be troubled less often and his ministers free to work on the issues which concern his service.

Pierre Grillon (ed.) (1975) *Les Papiers de Richelieu*, vol. 1. Paris: Pedone, pp. 141–2.

DOCUMENT 10   **THE PRINCE OF CONDÉ TO LOUIS XIII, 1626**

Condé, next in line to the throne after Louis XIII's brother, Gaston d'Orléans, was released from prison in 1619 where he had been sent for rebellion. Later, he took part in the royal campaigns against the Huguenots, whom he came to hate, in 1622. Here, he declares his loyalty to the king after a meeting with Cardinal Richelieu.

. . . I cannot but also express my fidelity to *monsieur* the Cardinal, who puts to one side all of his personal interests in order to support faithfully your own, never fearing in the process the accumulation of enemies. And on the resolve which he expressed to me to come to a settlement with *monseigneur* your brother, such as his stature merits, I dare say that I would have given you the same advice if you had not already taken it, because this will be very dear to you, the main pillar of your state and the strength of France principally until such time as God gives to you some children, for which I pray daily . . .

I do not doubt, also, that you know how to avoid all factions against your service, as you are obliged to do before God, among which my name will never be found, for I will remain with you always, resolutely for any and against any without any conditions. I offer you this and swear on the damnation of my soul, today as I took communion, and implore you to take heed of all the other things of which the Cardinal has spoken to me, which things he will tell you. I rely on him and will declare to you that my advice is very much like his own wishing nothing but to see Your Majesty reigning absolutely and everyone under you doing his part.

Pierre Grillon (ed.) (1975) *Les Papiers de Richelieu*, vol. 1. Paris: Pedone, p. 343.

DOCUMENT 11   **RICHELIEU ON DUELLING, 1626**

Richelieu explains why duelling must be forbidden.

All the theologians agree, for only one reason, that the duel cannot be permitted under God's law, but I have not seen any of them clearly express the real reason . . . [which is] that kings are not the absolute masters over people's lives and consequently cannot condemn them to death without them having committed a crime, which means that since the majority of their subjects who have a quarrel do not deserve death, they cannot therefore be permitted a duel which exposes them to this very end.

Pierre Grillon (ed.) (1975) *Les Papiers de Richelieu*, vol. 1. Paris: Pedone, p. 575.

DOCUMENT 12   **MEMOIR FROM THE PRINCE OF CONDÉ TO LOUIS XIII, OCTOBER 1627**

Apparently forgetting his earlier promise to defer to the advice of Richelieu, Condé offers his own suggesting the crown does all it can immediately to eradicate Protestantism throughout France through open war.

I believe, according to my conscience, that the king would do much better by openly attacking all the cities [of the Huguenots] at once rather than taking them one by one. And to conquer them, I think the following points are absolutely necessary. The first is to resolve to follow this plan and never to lay down arms until the king holds in his hands all that remains of the Huguenot towns. The second is to close your ears to any talk of a peace treaty and especially with the dukes of Rohan, Brison and other [Huguenot military leaders] who are only part of this faction for their own profit . . .

The cost of war is immense, the way it is fought now, and it is impossible to make it last for different reasons. The first is that the king's money does not ordinarily arrive on schedule though it arrives sooner or later; the other is that when there is none one must live off the land, and so there can be no discipline and war cannot last. Moreover, the enemies of the king have no other enemy apart from the king, being clear that Catholic towns, rural gentlemen, and most provincial governors get along with them, favouring the house, the brother, the relations of their servants. And so everyone looks after themselves and their own interests at the expense of the public and makes the king's affairs impossible.

In this way, everyone wants a garrison near them, not in order to defend themselves, but to put money into the bank. To bring a lasting solution to this and a swift end to that which remains in Languedoc [where the Huguenots remained strong], it seems to me that we must proceed in the following manner.

The first is to declare the dukes of Rohan, Brison, and the others involved enemies of the state; order without delay the confiscation of all the goods of those who follow them and have their houses demolished. It is not enough to talk about it; it must be done. And to this end we must conduct a census in each diocese of all the rebels and then demolish their homes.

Following from this, the Huguenots will do the same to the houses of the catholics, and then these beggars of money and of garrisons [promised according to the *brevets* of the Edict of Nantes], who want war for their profit to the detriment of the state, seeing war brought to them and their possessions destroyed, will wage war all the more earnestly in their own interests. As for these rebels, however, seeing that, instead of winning them what they wanted, rebellion costs them their ruin, they will change their minds and their opinions . . .

After, we must leave nothing for the rebels to pick over and destroy everything from city to city, burning their neighbours' houses and, in a word, proceeding with utter ruthlessness and while holding them in this poverty, with war everywhere, attack some of the ringleaders who will not be helped by anyone or with any money, everyone being out for themselves.

And to meet the expenses as cheaply as possible in the future, it is essential that, for one or two of the scheduled payments [to the armies], the king offers the money in advance, because this way, while this money lasts, we will conduct war with discipline, and meanwhile we can negotiate with the provinces to carry the expense to the relief of the king . . .

In closing, send to Languedoc very few troops from the region and plenty of foreigners, and having done so we will shortly see the end of the war and the king absolute master in all the cities. And, on this last point, could the governors not perform any function but under me, because otherwise they will contradict me on everything in order to favour each other . . .

Pierre Grillon (ed.) (1977) Les Papiers de Richelieu, vol. 2. Paris: Pedone, pp. 611–12.

DOCUMENT 13   MEMOIR FROM RICHELIEU TO MARIE DE MEDICI, MAY 1630

By stressing the need to go to war, Richelieu addresses the opposition of his two principal political adversaries in the months leading to the crucial Day of the Dupes, the Queen Mother herself and the Keeper of the Seals, Michel de Marillac.

All of the reasons put forward by the Keeper of the Seals make it clear that peace is to be desired. I have always thought so, for these same reasons, and I have never failed to think of ways of procuring it. Your Majesty and the Keeper of the Seals know well that in a memo that I sent to the king after the capture of Pinerolo I did not fail to point out the problems that would arise from the continuation of the war and the reasons for considering buying peace at the price of the restitution of Pinerolo. You know also that I received no other reply to the memo than that the king took the more noble side and went and attacked Savoy . . .

The reasons brought up by the Keeper of the Seals also make it clear that one cannot wage war without great hardship, which is true not just in this particular case but in all others, war being one of the scourges with which it pleases God to afflict man.

But it does not follow from this that one must bring peace on weak, low, and shameful conditions, since one would open oneself this way to much greater inconveniences than those of the present war.

The aversion which some people have to war is not a sufficient reason to bring such a peace, since often they feel and complain as much about necessary evils as those which one can avoid, and they are also as ignorant of that which is of value to the state as they are sensitive and eager to complain about the troubles that they must suffer in order to avoid even greater ones.

Whoever makes peace under shameful conditions will not keep it for long, will lose his reputation forever, and will expose himself in the future to long wars, being certain that no one will fear attacking us, considering the lack of constancy and resolve which we would have shown on this occasion where we have advantages that we will not enjoy again. All of the foreigners will consider our alliance useless because of our weakness and will not believe they can find security but with Spain, from whom they will voluntarily suffer their tyranny, in order to avoid their wicked intentions from which they will judge us unable to protect them.

Pierre Grillon (ed.) (1982) *Les Papiers de Richelieu*, vol. 5. Paris: Pedone, pp. 260–1.

DOCUMENT 14 RICHELIEU TO LOUIS XIII, 12 NOVEMBER 1630

Richelieu thanks the king for expressing his unequivocal position on the future direction of government policy on the so-called Day of the Dupes which isolated Michel de Marillac and Marie de Medici politically.

It is impossible for me to express to Your Majesty the extreme happiness that I felt yesterday with the honour of your vision. Your feelings are full of munificence and all the more worthy for having been submitted to reason and to the just considerations for the health and repose of your state. I implore you never to fear communicating them to your creatures and to believe that more and more they will work at realising them to your satisfaction and your advantage. I wish for your glory more than any servant has ever done for that of his master, and I will never forget what I can do to contribute to it. The remarkable testimonies which it pleased you yesterday to offer me from your kindness touched my heart. I feel so extraordinarily obliged that I cannot express it.

Pierre Grillon (ed.) (1982) *Les Papiers de Richelieu*, vol. 5. Paris: Pedone, p. 644.

DOCUMENT 15 AN ANONYMOUS WARNING TO LOUIS XIII, 1631

Cardinal Richelieu holds with the highest offices in France, the principal governorships; with the governorships, the strongest places, and the provinces, the ports and harbours; with these, the islands and the warships; with the warships, the cannons, and the soldiery; with the armaments, the finances; with the finances, absolute authority in your council.

Quoted in Alan James (2004) *The Navy and Government in Early Modern France, 1572–1661*. Woodbridge: Boydell Press, p. 75.

DOCUMENT 16 A POPULAR UPRISING IN BORDEAUX, 1635

The following is a report from a local official to the chancellor, Séguier, in Paris dated 20 May 1635 of a popular uprising in Bordeaux following the imposition of a new tax on wine.

Monseigneur, I feel a certain regret for not having earlier brought to your attention the sedition which arrived in this city last Monday over the establishment of a tax that the King ordered to be raised each year on tavern keepers. The disorder was so extraordinary this time that it was impossible to find the opportunity or the leisure to write . . . [T]he agent who was responsible for establishing the said tax and an individual, named Desaigues, who made it his business to carry a sword and meddled in the affair without having any authority from the city hall, were both killed at different times and in different places having left the said city hall in disguises in order to save themselves. Two or three others were also killed . . . as was another, named Emery, who was commissioned to raise the said tax. And it is remarkable that those involved in the sedition did not pillage or steal anything and that even after having killed the said Emery in his home, they did not take a penny . . . They also demanded the lives of two judicial officials who were in the said city hall, and one of them who was wearing a hat was told that life did not require that type of ceremony and took it off him. They then put hoods over their shoulders and led them to their lodgings where, having put them, they cried 'long live the king'. I am told they also cried 'long live the king' after having killed one of those taken for a *gabeleur* [a hated collector of the *gabelle* tax]. The next day, which was Tuesday, they were in the city armed like the day before and cried again on various occasions 'long live the king', and many among them claimed that they would pay His Majesty anything he would like to impose on them as long as it was not on wine.

This public tragedy stems from the judicial officials not being supported by the bourgeois as they claimed they would . . . The judicial officials and captains told me at the chateau du Ha, where I retreated, that they could not find any bourgeois to oppose the seditious elements, which some of the *messieurs* of the parlement confirmed who had been responsible for assembling them.

I returned with the members of the parlement to the palace, where having reported that I had written to [the Duke of] Épernon and asked his advice as early as the Monday after dinner about the said sedition and that he had sent me response by the captain of the guards by which he informed me that he could not come so promptly, as much because of his illness as because he was not well guarded, it was instantly decided by the assembled bodies to send two deputies to the said *sieur* d'Épernon to plead with him to come promptly in the hope that his presence would end the disorder. Following this plea the said *sieur* d'Épernon arrived last Thursday and came to the city hall where, upon his entry he dismissed the judicial officials and forbade them from fulfilling their charges until His Majesty otherwise orders and later brought such order to the city that since his arrival the seditious have remained closed up in their homes so that the city appears to be in peace.

Boris Porchnev (ed.) (1963) *Les soulèvements populaires en France, de 1623 à 1648.* Paris: SEVPEN, pp. 586–7.

DOCUMENT 17 **RICHELIEU TO THE BARON OF CHARNACÉ, NOVEMBER 1635**

Early in the war with Spain, Richelieu sent this letter to Charnacé, who was with the army in Flanders and who had some authority to conduct negotiations, to ensure that the Dutch did not come to a separate settlement with Spain.

[T]hey are too wise and too clear-sighted not to recognise that a separate treaty or peace would be much less advantageous to them and secure than a general one, where the interests of all the allies are included and settled. Even though it might appear that by treating with them alone they might get better conditions, these would come at great cost in time, as you have already suggested to them. I am not surprised that the Spaniards are looking to come to a settlement with the members of the Estates [of the United Dutch Provinces] and to try to get them to separate their interests from ours, since that is the only way they have to achieve their ends. But I would be astonished if these members, who are aware of the serious obligations that they have always had towards France and who have to this point very wisely deflected the effects of the wicked designs of the House of Austria, were to abandon the king on this occasion to the detriment of their treaties, their faith, and their own interests. Whatever happens, you may assure them that His Majesty is determined not to entertain any accommodation except in concert and in agreement with all of his allies . . .

In a word, from a separate treaty many accidents could arise, and none is to be feared with a common treaty, where security would be complete.

We are quite certain that if we conduct the peace negotiations well, the fear that is held of the domination and tyranny of the House of Austria will lead many people who appear on their side to come over to ours.

M. Avenel (ed.) (1863) *Lettres instructions diplomatiques et papiers d'état du Cardinal de Richelieu*, vol. 5. Paris: Imprimerie Impériale, pp. 340–2.

DOCUMENT 18 **A CIRCULAR LETTER FROM THE KING TO THE BISHOPS OF FRANCE, JULY 1636**

Much of the draft of this document was written in Richelieu's own hand.

It is with regret that I must inform you of the disorders which [the enemy] commits throughout Lorraine and on my frontiers, that they have burned churches, overturned altars, spilled the blood of priests, by all means impious and sacrilegious ended divine worship in many places. This deplorable subject leads me to send this order so that according to the ancient customs of France you will require of all secular and regular clergy and of my other subjects in your dioceses the conduct of public and private prayers to God for the well-being and tranquillity of this church, that of all of Christianity, and particularly of the kingdom which I desire principally so that I may have the means to execute quickly my determination to relieve my people.

M. Avenel (ed.) (1863) *Lettres instructions diplomatiques*
et papiers d'état du Cardinal de Richelieu,
vol. 5. Paris: Imprimerie Impériale, pp. 500–1.

DOCUMENT 19	A MEMOIR FROM RICHELIEU TO A REPRESENTATIVE IN ROME AND TO THE POPE'S REPRESENTATIVE IN PARIS, APRIL 1637

Richelieu insists that the pope's refusal to recognise Protestant powers will make it impossible to end the war.

If His Holiness [the pope] continues to negotiate peace as he has begun to do, we will never see the end of the negotiations nor the beginning of the treaty which he wishes to arrange.

For negotiations for peace to begin, it is necessary for all the deputies to be there. For them to be there, it is necessary for them to have been invited and to be guaranteed safe passage and for the intermediaries not to appear suspect to them.

The Swedes have not been invited by anyone and do not wish to come as much for this reason as because the pope has indicated that he does not wish his ministers to work with Protestants. His designs are justly held in suspicion by them . . .

The [papal] legate, the negotiator, is not trusted by any of the Protestants and what is more he is unable to work with them since the pope will not permit it, and consequently it is clear that in continuing to talk of peace as one does we will never see it. These problems must be pointed out in the strongest terms to the pope . . .

M. Avenel (ed.) (1863) *Lettres instructions diplomatiques et papiers d'état du*
Cardinal de Richelieu, vol. 5. Paris: Imprimerie Impériale, pp. 765–6.

DOCUMENT 20 THE DUKE D'ÉPERNON TO THE CHANCELLOR, SÉGUIER, JUNE 1637

The Duke of Épernon offers his thoughts on a popular uprising.

Monsieur, although I have not recovered my strength and at my age it is not easy to recover from an illness as serious as the one I have suffered, I nevertheless make this effort to serve the king in the present affairs and prefer to risk what little health remains than to spare my attention from matters arising. I am certain, Monsieur, that you have learned what my son the duc de La Valette has very successfully executed in Angoumois and Perigord and that he has in this way dispelled the strongest faction that has formed for a long time in this state by an uprising of the people, without the enemy being able to profit in any way from our troubles, by the good order he left in the army before leaving the frontier. The lack of success that the people had has certainly snatched their arms from their hands, but not the rage, nor the ill-will from their hearts, no less than the rash and seditious words from their mouths, such that being in this state I am far from imploring the grace, or the clemency of the king in their favour. I believe, on the contrary, that it is very necessary to keep them in fear, to threaten those who have failed in, or who might yet neglect, their duty with the confiscation of their property and the razing of their houses, and to make a special commission because this revolt, being supported by many well-off people who have much to lose, it might be enough to contain them in this way and to keep them from returning to their previous fury. I make this proposal out of the passion I have for the service of the king. You will advise by your prudence, *monsieur*, what will be expedient in this matter which is one of the most important and dangerous that has come up in a long time and which we owe principally to the impunity of the people of Saintonge . . .

Boris Porchnev (ed.) (1963) *Les Soulèvements populaires en France, de 1623 à 1648*. Paris: SEVPEN, p. 603.

DOCUMENT 21 THE PRELATE IN THE ARMY, 1638

Henri d'Escoubleau de Sourdis was the archbishop of Bordeaux and also commander of the navy. Here, he makes the case that there is no conflict between serving the church and serving the king in war.

It is true that sovereign pontiffs have pronounced some rules forbidding clergymen from bearing weapons and take as their authority the words of the gospel in which Jesus Christ commanded Saint Peter to sheathe his sword which he had been using with justice and zeal for his own defence . . . Without wishing to challenge the authority of these popes or deny the humble respect that we owe to their rulings, there is no doubt that if weapons were forbidden to clerics solely on the basis of the rules of Jean VIII or of Innocent, with the writings of Saint Ambrose, this could only be taken as rules towards a voluntary perfection and not as a fundamental duty, in consideration of the terms with which they are written. Tradition, which is the legitimate inter-pretation of laws, has shown us the truth of this . . . [T]he sovereign pontiffs have taken them as their own in this way, as proved by their practice to the contrary . . . I draw the conclusion that clerics can, in their current condition and for the defence of their provinces, do as the popes have done in Italy for its defence.

. . . If all bishops may go to war and join armies, those of France are obliged to do so . . . There are those in this country who are blind to, or are ignorant of, the extent of the piety of our kings; it has been made obvious in the valuable gifts they have made to the church . . . [A]nd they claim with their offerings to be doing their duty to the divine majesty, in recognition that from Him alone do they hold their sceptre and their crown . . . [I]t is certain that fulfilling this duty does not detract from the glory which our kings have earned, with their presents of so many fine fiefs, such noble lands, this great number of seigneurial rights which the church now holds and which are kept in such brilliance by its main body, the bishops.

. . . That is why the bishops of this kingdom, who are of the second order . . . have always paid hommage to our kings and rendered customary duties, no more and no less than the other vassals who have always done so.

Eugène Sue (ed.) (1830) *Correspondance de Henri d'Escoubleau de Sourdis*,
vol. 3. Paris: Crapelet, pp. 134–5, 140, and 142–3.

DOCUMENT 22   **A CIRCULAR LETTER FROM THE KING TO THE BISHOPS OF FRANCE, FEBRUARY 1641**

Richelieu intends to establish Jesuit missions.

As my cousin the cardinal of Richelieu is not content with relieving my burdens with his constant care and vigils for the greater advantage and glory of this state but, from a piety and charity worthy of his high office in the church and from his zeal for the public good, also directs his thoughts to anything that might glorify God and the spiritual well-being of my subjects, having told me of the plan he has to establish missions of fathers of the Company of Jesus [Jesuits] throughout my kingdom where they can be em-ployed usefully in the education and edification of my subjects and to provide from his own wealth the cost of these missions so that there will be no imposition or charge to the people . . . I heartily endorse such a laudable and useful establishment. And, though I do not doubt that you are also inclined to help it succeed in whatever way you can, nevertheless I very much wish to indicate with this letter how thoroughly I hope to see the good effects that we can expect from this and that my intention is that, to this end, you will accept, without any hindrance, the fathers from the said company who will be sent into your dioceses by their superiors to conduct their missions and that you will give them all the assistance and support in these things that your authority allows . . .

M. Avenel (ed.) (1867) *Lettres instructions diplomatiques et papiers d'état du Cardinal de Richelieu*, vol. 6. Paris: Imprimerie Impériale, pp. 751–2.

DOCUMENT 23   **RICHELIEU TO LOUIS XIII, MAY 1642**

Since it pleases His Majesty to take an interest in what happens to me, I will tell you frankly that I cannot predict but that the end of my illness will take a long time and that, although the doctors and surgeons tell me often that my ills are not getting worse, I do not feel the improvement that they have been promising me daily for the last month. Whatever end it pleases the Lord to bring to my illness I will accept it, God willing, with patience and will be very happy as long as I know that Your Majesty is well and that he takes Perpignan. These are now the two things that concern me most . . .

M. Avenel (ed.) (1867) *Lettres instructions diplomatiques et papiers d'état du Cardinal de Richelieu*, vol. 6. Paris: Imprimerie Impériale, p. 924.

DOCUMENT 24   **THE *TESTAMENT POLITIQUE* OF CARDINAL RICHELIEU**

An often-quoted section from the opening of the testament politique, *dedicated to the king, Louis XIII, and said to have been written for him by Richelieu to provide advice and inspiration after his death which came in December 1642.*

When Your Majesty decided to give me, at one and the same time, a place on your council and special confidence for the direction of your affairs, I can say in honesty that the huguenots shared the state with you, that the high nobility conducted themselves as if they were not your subjects, and the most powerful governors of the provinces as if they were sovereign in their lands . . . Despite all the difficulties that I outlined to Your Majesty, knowing what kings can achieve when they apply their power, I dared to promise you, without being rash in my opinion, that you would find a remedy to the disorder of your state and that, in a short time, your prudence, your strength, and the blessing of

God would give a new look to this kingdom. I promised that I would employ all of my industry and all of the authority that it pleased Your Majesty to give me to ruin the huguenot faction, to tame the pride of the nobility, reduce all of your subjects to their duty and to lift your name among the other countries to the position it ought to hold . . .

Louis André (ed.) (1947) *Cardinal Richelieu: Testament Politique.*
Paris: Laffont, pp. 93–5.

DOCUMENT 25   **MAZARIN TO ABEL SERVIEN, 14 AUGUST 1648**

Mazarin reflects on the negotiations that would lead to the Peace of Westphalia and defends himself, in this period of domestic difficulties, against widespread criticism.

It would be impossible, either now or any time in the future, for me to display more passion for the conclusion of peace than I always have; but there may come a time when this state will need it more than ever. You know the truth of the first and you can foresee the second, like me, by reflecting on what has happened in this kingdom over the last few months. Never has the concord been stronger, thanks be to God, within the royal family. Never have our affairs been in such a promising state and led us to hope for more advantages over our enemies, if they decide to continue the war, or for better conditions for this crown, if they are resolved finally for peace. But, to be sure, I can see, and I cry tears of blood, that while prospects on the outside appear so bright, at the same time the inside is extraordinarily rotten and that by some deplorable fatalism we are in the process of bringing upon ourselves the very harm that our enemies have failed to bring. There is almost no part of our body that is not daily corrupted and someone among *les grands* [the great nobility] who would think themselves more respected and their affairs better served if there was disorder, starting already to cause trouble, and thinking themselves able to profit from the situation to demand and to claim anything at all. The parlements of the kingdom believe, in imitation of that of Paris, that they can do anything and order with impunity anything they see to their advantage, and the lower courts also are daring to ape the others. From all directions, one only hears of disobedience or violence against the crown's farmers or those charged with the collection of money.

The people are beginning to get a taste for the comforts and the hopes that they have been maliciously given from having paid almost nothing at all. And, the only possible remedy for this sickness being violence, sometimes much worse than the illness itself, the well-intentioned are few in number and unable to do much. The ill-intentioned find it easy to spread their venom and their wicked ideas because they prove useful to the people who hear them. And while I work myself to death, day and night, for the glory of this crown and for the individual happiness of each Frenchman, the enemies of the state and those who hate me . . . maliciously sow the idea among the people that I have amassed treasures and sent them to Italy, while in truth, without a word of exaggeration, I borrow every day just to have enough to live on and to maintain my household. It is, moreover, from wickedness that they undertake to make me odious with the people who are easily taken in, not caring to penetrate beneath the surface, and above all they attack me principally because I am a foreigner.

Chéruel, A. (ed.) (1883) *Lettres du cardinal de Mazarin*, vol. 3. Paris: Imprimerie Nationale, pp. 173–5.

DOCUMENT 26 TURENNE TO HIS SISTER, MADEMOISELLE DE BOUILLON, 9 DECEMBER 1648

Turenne's brother, the Duke of Bouillon, was disgraced and exiled for his role in a plot against Richelieu in 1642. This caused many problems for the family. In this letter to his sister of 1648 from the field, Turenne makes clear his determination to press (through a trusted agent in the capital named Pâris) for high personal office and for the restitution of the stature of his family as reward for his military service.

My dear sister, I have received your letters . . . I am deciphering them as quickly as possible. You will have heard from Pâris how my feelings are precisely the same as yours. I can at least assure you now that they are very firm.

  Monsieur le Cardinal [Mazarin] wrote to me today about the complaints made by my sister-in-law. I responded that it was no surprise at all that she is aggrieved, my brother's situation not having been resolved. I am entirely in agreement with this person about my voyage and about pressing either to breaking point or to see our household in the position in which it ought to be and myself with a suitable charge, as long as there is no trickery involved.

  Pâris will do absolutely nothing but that which you ask of him. I am writing to my brother and to my sister-in-law. I can assure you that from my side I will always be closely involved. May we hold firm in demanding for me that which was in your cipher [or coded letter], which is exactly what Pâris has been commissioned for, or otherwise declare clearly that I can no longer remain the servant of *Monsieur le Cardinal*. We must not fear the outcome, the future is in the hands of God.

Huart, Suzanne d' (ed.) (1971) *Lettres de Turenne*. Paris: SEVPEN, p. 458.

DOCUMENT 27   FROM THE MEMOIRS OF THE CARDINAL OF RETZ, DECEMBER 1648

The Cardinal de Retz, who would later become a leading frondeur, *reflects on the danger to the state posed by the parlement and the people of Paris at the beginning of the Fronde.*

Your highness [Condé] told me recently that this disposition of the people was nothing but smoke; but this smoke, so black and so thick, is kept up by a fire that is very lively and well-lit. The parlement fans it, and this parlement, with the best and even the simplest intentions in the world, is very capable of stoking it to a point where it will flare up and consume itself but which in the meantime will threaten, more than once, the state . . . Had the parlement responded . . . to the ridiculous and pernicious proposition that the Cardinal made to declare whether they claimed to put limits on royal authority, if, I say, the wisest of that body had not avoided the question, France, in my opinion, would have been out of luck, because [the parlement] declaring the affirmative, as it was about to do, would have lifted the cloak that covers the mystery of the state. Each monarchy has its own. That of France consists of this religious or sacred silence in which one shrouds, by almost always blindly obeying kings, the right, which one is not even willing to believe one has, to exempt oneself . . . It is a miracle that the parlement has not just lifted this cloak, and has not lifted it formally and by decree, which would be of more dangerous consequence and more fatal than the liberty the people have taken, for some time now, to see through it.

Cardinal de Retz (1987) *Mémoires*, vol. I. *1613–1649.*
Paris: Éditions Garnier, pp. 343–4.

DOCUMENT 28   A MAZARINADE OF 1650

The Mazarinades were a series of political pamphlets which poured from the Parisian presses during the Fronde expressing all manner of grievances, though a near universal hatred of Mazarin himself was one common feature. This is a poster, in the form of a death sentence, that appeared with portraits of Mazarin hung in effigy.

Jules Mazarin: For having, by his artifices, many times failed to conclude a general peace. For having had various assassinations committed, of which with sufficient proof he is charged with being the sole author. For having denuded and transported out of France the king's coffers. For having wanted to starve the city of Paris and sacrifice the bourgeois of it to his hatred. For having secretly taken the grain of the kingdom and sold it to the enemies of the state. For by his spells and his charms subordinated the spirit of the Queen. For having violated the customs of France and transgressed all of the laws both divine and human. For having been recognised as the author of the civil wars which have been for two years in France. For having made impositions on the subjects of the king and tyrannically extorted from them immense sums. Finally, all of the above specified, having been proven and verified by all of the parlements of France and moreover having been charged with the crime of treason of the highest order, has been condemned to be hanged and strangled by the hand of the executioner, and for not having yet been able to seize and apprehend his person, his portrait has been attached to the gallows and displayed over twenty-four hours, in common areas, public places and all places destined for the execution of criminals, that is in the place de Grève, at the porte de Paris, at the Croix du Tiroir, at Les Halles, at the place Maubert and at the end of the Pont Neuf, the present warrant executed, read, published and posted at Paris, the third of November 1650.

From Hubert Carrier (1989) *La Presse de la Fronde (1648–1653): Les Mazarinades, la conquête de l'opinion.* Geneva: Droz, p. 350.

DOCUMENT 29 **THE PRINCE OF CONDÉ TO THE PARLEMENT OF DIJON, 8 JULY 1651**

'Le grand Condé' explains his departure from court.

I thought it important for the service of the king to explain to you the reasons I have withdrawn from the court, and what has happened since I have been here at St Maur, so that my enemies and those of the state cannot offer a skewed interpretation of my actions . . .

Cardinal Mazarin, having had enough sway over the Queen to make her consent to my detention, has continued, through the intermediary of his creatures, to poison His Majesty against me, and, without reflecting on the terrible consequences of my imprisonment and the disorders which he has caused in the state, we have seen them practising the same artifices as before my arrest.

Rumours have been spread among the people to discredit me; my most innocent actions have been slandered, and the indifferent ones maliciously interpreted against me. Not content with grooming the people with bad impressions which they have wanted to make of my conduct, the creatures of Cardinal Mazarin have acted within the government; they have worked on the Queen and have wanted to encourage negotiations with anyone they felt was not favourable to me, hoping to gain an advantage over me and that this plotting would facilitate their designs. They have already begun to act on the king; and the interest that you have taken in my liberty, and the judgment that you subsequently made against the author of my imprisonment, have been slandered as faction and intrigue. They have wanted to present your acts of justice as working against royal authority and have condemned the parlements in order to vindicate Cardinal Mazarin and to predispose the king to his return once he reaches his majority, to the prejudice of your cause, of the interest you have in upholding your decrees, and of public order, which can only be guaranteed by his absence . . .

A few days before our departure, we were warned by many people, of a design that they had against us . . . We would have continued to live with the suspicions and mistrust, the decision to leave being very difficult to take, had we not been warned, the very night of our departure, that they were going to execute it and that, to this end, the soldiers of the Regiment of the Guards had been ordered to assemble with their colours and had we not seen many troops in various places . . . The Prince of Conti, my brother, himself declared to the company the need we had to guard ourselves from the sort of activity which we had already experienced; that this was the only motive for our retreat, and to prevent in this way the sort of disorders that such violence would have caused in the state; that we have no other claims, neither for ourselves nor for our friends; and that we demand only the security that people of our birth should get from the king whilst serving him faithfully as we have always done and as we insist we will do for the rest of our lives; this not being possible until the banishment of the creatures of Cardinal Mazarin removes all hope of his return, and re-establishing the trust necessary to reform the royal household and for public order we declared to his royal highness and to the members of the parlement of Paris that as soon as the *sieurs* Servien, Le Tellier and Lionne are removed we will not fail to come to their majesties in order to continue our service to the king and to the state. And we can assure you that a declaration this disinterested and advantageous to France was received by his royal highness and by the parlement of Paris as favourably as we could have hoped.

Le duc d'Aumale (ed.) (1892) *Histoire des princes de Condé*,
vol. 6. Paris: Lévy, pp. 489–92.

DOCUMENT 30   **A MAZARINADE OF 1651**

From the good and true Frenchmen, faithful and obedient servants and sub-jects of the sacred person of the King, father of the people, faithful servants too of the princes of the blood his children, and conservators of the crown and other good and faithful officers and men of justice, aides and supporters of the same; mortal enemies of the impious, scoundrel, traitor, thief, tyrant, sacrilegious, perturber of the public, sorcerer, magician, pervert, monopolist, transvestite and reprehensible monster Jules Mazarin, Italian, renegade, standard bearer of the Anti-Christ and of the hereafter named accomplices, adherents, and ill-doers of his.

It is required of Servien, Lionne and Le Tellier, factionnaries and accomplices of the said Mazarin, to vacate the city of Paris within twenty-four hours, and within eight days the kingdom, so that henceforth God will be served, adored and honoured by the re-establishment everywhere of the Christian religion, the eternal union of their majesties with the said princes of the blood, the conclusion of the general peace so much desired by the princes and by the poor people, kept by the said Servien, Le Tellier and Lionne from relief and peace, and finally that the sun of justice might shine again, which since so long has been almost entirely eclipsed, all by the tyranny and theft of the said Mazarin, Servien, Lionne and Le Tellier, who want nothing but trouble, the loss of the princes and of the kingdom; and, failing this, it is declared by the said good and faithful Frenchmen that they will employ what little is left them, together with their natural strength, hoping and assuring themselves of the divine abundance of supernatural forces, to make amends for this quarrel with the aid, comfort and good council of the princes of the blood, to purge the state and cut out the roots of all these infernal monsters above, and other factionnaries of the said impious, scoundrel, traitor, thief, monopolist, seducer, homosexual, transvestite, rogue and infernal monster Mazarin.

From Hubert Carrier (1989) *La Presse de la Fronde (1648–1653): Les Mazarinades, la conquête de l'opinion*. Geneva: Droz, p. 346.

DOCUMENT 31   **A FORMAL STATEMENT ISSUED BY THE ORMÉE OF BORDEAUX, 16 MAY 1652**

The self-styled 'Ormée' issued this statement in reaction to an order by the parlement in the city for them to disband.

Upon the news received by the men of the Ormée, assembled for the service of the king and of *monsieur* the prince [Condé], of an edict by the parlement of this city, abusive and unreasonable, intended to hinder and shackle the fair designs of the said faithful assembly, we declare that if the said edict is published in the said city, that the authors, adherents, and accomplices of the said edict will be pursued, forbidding the said parlement, on the pain of death, from taking such action in the future, in opposition to which the said Ormée will take up arms, pleading and exhorting the most faithful bourgeois of the city to lend a hand, on the threat of being declared traitors to their patrimony and as such banished in perpetuity from the city with their goods confiscated.

From *Les Archives historiques de la Gironde*, vol. 8 (1866), p. 385.

DOCUMENT 32   A REPORT FROM THE ORMÉE, 20 MAY 1652

With a royal army approaching the city of Bordeaux, the 'Ormée' declares its optimism and its defiance.

You will no doubt be surprised by our fronde of the ormée and its power to disband the parlement and to stop it from exercising justice. This is something that the king, with his power and all of his declarations, has not been able to achieve. This is not all. We claim to have suppressed their charges, to have abolished venality, and to administer justice by men of probity and known ability. This is the first step in the reformation of the ills of this city which we undertake through the inspiration of the Holy Spirit. I pray it brings our work to a happy end. Seriously, I will tell you that we would have difficulty backing down from the two propositions which have already been debated at the last assemblies of the fronde: the first, to take account of the enormous sums already raised during the early troubles, under whatever name; the second, to have a general appeal concerning all the affairs of the bourgeois of this city; to which end we have joined to our assembly the judges and men of the money-markets and sent our deputies at first light to make our appeal. I understand that the major proportion of the bourgeoisie will join with us and that they have indicated their union, so well endowed are we with the good government of our senators.

From *Les Archives historiques de la Gironde*, vol. 8 (1866), p. 386.

DOCUMENT 33   LE TELLIER TO TURENNE ON AN OFFER OF PEACE TO CONDÉ, 26 SEPTEMBER 1652

[T]he king has commanded me to inform you that, Monsieur the prince [of Condé] having enquired of the Cardinal to work with their majesties for the pacification of the troubles, they have allowed M. l'abbé Fouquet [brother of Nicolas Fouquet] to go to Paris with the authority to sign a treaty on the following conditions: that everything will be returned to the state it was in before the troubles; thereupon that all places and governments taken by the party of the princes will be returned . . . without demolishing the fortifications; that the king will grant a million *livres* to M. the prince to distribute to those of his party who have suffered, and beyond that will grant forgiveness to some of his friends, who are those who you will have heard about already. But because M. the prince does not wish to renounce his treaty with Spain before reasonable conditions are offered to them for a general peace, which the king will negotiate, the said abbé Fouquet has been ordered to arrange with him that the troops that were under his command, and that of the Duke of Angien, before the present disorders will remain as they are in the quarters that will be ordered without serving in the army of His Majesty until such time as the Spaniards have agreed to the peace on the said conditions or, having refused, M. the prince has renounced the treaty that he made with them and until the restitution of the places and governments has taken place. And although we cannot imagine that he could have any difficulty with this arrangement, still, knowing as we do the capriciousness of the character of M. the prince, we cannot predict what will happen.

Le duc d'Aumale (ed.) (1892) *Histoire des princes de Condé*,
vol. 6. Paris: Lévy, pp. 566–7.

DOCUMENT 34   TURENNE TO HIS WIFE, 7 JANUARY 1653

I believe that the poor weather and the lack of supplies will mean the armies will have to retire . . . At the moment we are besieging Château-Porcien.

You have been wondering about the reprimand that I am preparing to give you. It is that my sister tells me that you have been going to sleep so late that it could affect your health. If you had seen my letter, you would know that I am unhappy with you going out to assemblies or to the ball. I pray you seriously, out of love for me, to go to bed at a good hour and to avoid anything that might make you ill. I will have spies watching and will know well how you act in the future. I can assure you that nothing in the world is more dear to me.

It is certain that, God willing, I will soon be in Paris and will have great joy at seeing you . . . It can only be that *Monsieur le Cardinal* [Mazarin] will go at the first opportunity to Paris where everything is back in order. I can assure that I press and will continue to press as far as possible my own affairs. I seem to recall having seen in one of your letters, but I cannot find where, that you spoke to me of buying a house in Paris. I find that very appropriate and anything that you can do, my sister and you, so that we become very rich. Indeed I will be very happy to have a house in Paris and, since I hope soon to be there, I pray you to complete it without me. I am not certain whether I have imagined that you asked me about this or if it is true. Send my regards to my dear sister. I am yours with all my heart.

Huart, Suzanne d' (ed.) (1971) *Lettres de Turenne*.
Paris: SEVPEN, p. 489.

DOCUMENT 35   MAZARIN TO LOUIS XIV, 17 SEPTEMBER 1659

Your letter of the 14th fills me with joy, more and more, seeing that nothing could add to the steadfastness with which you demonstrate your resolve to do the things which could contribute to your glory, to your tranquility, and to make you happy. I wish for nothing more in the world than this, and I hope that God will so grant me; because I think I can foresee that you will easily be your own master when you wish it . . . I will finish this by telling you, and the Queen, that the idea of having the superintendent [Fouquet] brought here is not because there is anything wrong, because I would have told you about it, but that if the month of October passes without first having given the orders for the renewal of the tax farms, and for a number of other things concerning the finances which the peace has given the opportunity to exploit advantageously, you would lose many millions and it would be impossible to survive next year. That is the only reason we must examine and come to an understanding with the superintendent about what he has to do . . .

Georges d'Avenel (ed.) (1906) *Lettres du cardinal Mazarin*,
vol. 9. Paris: Imprimerie Nationale, pp. 310–11.

DOCUMENT 36   **FOUQUET TO MAZARIN, 6 JANUARY 1660**

I saw M. Colbert, who came to see me at my home, and I told him that I felt obliged to defend myself to Your Eminence against many things which I have heard that he has accused me of, and that I am certain that in my place he would not have been able to do any less, but that this did not stop me from holding him in esteem . . . I added that I was certain that if he knew my intentions better he might not have criticised my methods and that . . . I wished his friendship and that we might work together on the execution of your orders . . .

Pierre Clément (ed.) (1861) *Lettres, instructions et mémoires de Colbert*,
vol. 1. Paris: Imprimerie Impériale, p. 518.

DOCUMENT 37   **MAZARIN TO FOUQUET, 14 FEBRUARY 1660**

Let me first say how delighted I am to learn of the increase that you have been able to get from the tax farms, beyond even what you and I had hoped for . . . and it is clear that you have brought all of the care, skill, and application to this that one has come to expect from someone as zealous and intelligent as you are . . .

Continue, therefore, to work with the same determination, and along with the merit that you acquire from having contributed to the flourishing of the kingdom, you should expect to receive signs of the goodwill of the king who will respond to the service that you render him.

Georges d'Avenel (ed.) (1906) *Lettres du cardinal Mazarin*,
vol. 9. Paris: Imprimerie Nationale, pp. 500–1.

DOCUMENT 38   A MEMOIR DICTATED BY LOUIS XIV, 9 MARCH 1661

A reflection on the lessons that Louis XIV claims Mazarin taught him before his death. An editorial note suggests that it was unfinished.

Monsieur le Cardinal [Mazarin] sensing the approach of his end, and wishing to be rid of the affairs of this world in order to concentrate fully on eternity, offered the final moments of his temporal life in the love that he had always had for the good of my state and for my particular glory. And, with this in mind, he left me much important advice which I have recollected as well as I could, among which as follows:

Firstly, to maintain the church with all its rights, immunities, and privileges, as befits the eldest son, without allowing it to be weakened under any circumstances; that I was obliged so by conscience; and also to take care that those to whom I give benefices have the ability, the piety, and the other qualities necessary . . .

With regard to the nobility, that it was my right arm, that I should value it, and to treat it with confidence and benevolence in all encounters.

That for the magistracy it was right to honour it but that it was very important to try to ensure that those of this profession do not get out of hand and to oblige them to stick within the limits of their duties . . .

That, from all that is required of a good king, I was obliged to relieve my people, not just from the *taille*, but from all other burdens . . .

That I had around me very capable and entirely faithful servants; that it was up to me to decide what each one was best suited to do and to employ them according to their talents.

That I must ensure that everyone is persuaded that I am the master; that favours should be sought from me alone; and especially not to distribute them to anyone but those who deserve it through their service, and their ability, and by their attachment to my person alone.

That I should take care to ensure that everyone on my council is on good terms for fear that their divisions could only prejudice my service; to listen to their advice on issues; always seek the best from among their different opinions; to make up my own mind and afterwards to remain determined, to retain my resolve, without allowing the smallest opportunity for any blow to my authority.

That if any among those who I employ in my service is unfortunate enough to undertake something without my order, I must absolutely remove them as unworthy to serve me.

That I must never suffer any scandal in my court, nor tolerate licentious ways; that I am obliged to this by God, and that even by the things of this world it befits my honour . . .

Pierre Clément (ed.) (1861) *Lettres, instructions et mémoires de Colbert*, vol. 1. Paris: Imprimerie Impériale, pp. 535–6.

DOCUMENT 39   THE EARLY DAYS OF THE PERSONAL REIGN OF LOUIS XIV

An extract from a letter of a Dutch observer at the French court, 18 March 1661.

... [P]eople here, since the death of the cardinal, speak with praise and even with admiration of the resolve of the king to take charge of the government. It is said that the king only makes use of the three ministers who I named in a previous letter, that is: the superintendent [Fouquet], Le Tellier, and Lionne, for advice, from the first on finance, from the second on matters relating to war, and from the third on foreign affairs, and not in order to form a private council to the exclusion of everyone else and in this way to give them the opportunity to take on board the direction of affairs. Everyone is unanimous that it is unbelievable with what promptitude and sharpness, what judgment and spirit this young prince treats and expedites his business which he accomplishes with great gentleness towards those with whom he has dealings and with much patience while listening to what one has to say to him, all of which wins him people's hearts. He expresses himself with great strength and, when it is needed, with an eloquence which surprises those who hear him talking about affairs either in the council, or elsewhere, and who had previously seen the cardinal [Mazarin] so absolutely the master of everything.

Jean de Boislisle (ed.) (1905) *Mémoriaux du conseil de 1661*,
vol. 1. Paris: Renouard, pp. 363–4.

WHO'S WHO

Anne of Austria   Spanish princess, wife to Louis XIII and mother to Louis XIV, headed the regency government with Mazarin during her son's minority, 1643–51.

Bernard of Saxe-Weimar   successful military entrepreneur in French service in Germany in the Thirty Years' War; died in 1639.

Charles IV, Duke of Lorraine   hostile to France, conspired with Gaston d'Orléans provoking French occupation of Lorraine.

Colbert, Jean-Baptiste   powerful minister with wide responsibilities during the personal rule of Louis XIV from 1661–85.

Concini, Carlo, Marshal Ancre   Italian favourite of Marie de Medici, dominated the regency council until his assassination in April 1617.

Condé, Henri II de Bourbon, Prince of (1588–1646)   prince of the blood and high-ranking noble who played an important political and military role from a young age. The focus of noble rebellion in the early seventeenth century, Condé then confirmed his loyalty and fought with the crown against the Huguenots.

Condé, Louis II de Bourbon, Duke of Enghien and Prince of (1621–86)   son of previous. Victor at Rocroi in 1643, known as 'the Great Condé' for his military leadership. Embodied the virtues of nobility. Led the latter stages of the Fronde against the government.

Épernon, Jean-Louis de Nogaret de La Valette, Duke of   powerful, independent noble, and veteran of the Wars of Religion, fought against Henri IV. For laying down his arms against Louis XIII he received the governorship of his native Guyenne which he held until his death in 1642. Succeeded by his son, Bernard de Nogaret de La Valette. Neither was trusted by Richelieu.

Fouquet, Nicolas   Superintendent of Finance from 1653. Disgraced in 1661 to make way for Colbert.

Gaston d'Orléans   brother to Louis XIII. Heir presumptive until 1638. Focus of noble discontent and rebellion.

Gustavus Adolphus   Protestant King of Sweden, successful in Thirty Years' War against Catholic Hapsburg Emperor Ferdinand II. Received subsidies from France before its formal entry into the war in 1635.

Henri IV   King of France (1589–1610) King of Navarre and former Huguenot military leader. Crowned king of France in 1594, a year after his conversion to Catholicism. Assassinated in 1610.

La Valette, Bernard de Nogaret de, Duke of Épernon   favoured son of Jean-Louis de Nogaret de La Valette whom he succeeded as Duke of Épernon. Disgraced with his father by Richelieu after the failure at the siege of Fuenterrabia in 1638.

La Valette, Louis de Nogaret, Cardinal of   brother of previous. Archbishop of Toulouse and cardinal. Commanded French armies and, unlike his father, loyal to Richelieu.

Le Tellier, Michel   Intendant of the army, then Secretary of State for War from 1645. Hated by many frondeurs. Loyal to Mazarin, helped to disgrace Fouquet. Responsible for many reforms in the army.

Louis XIII   King of France (1610–43) Son of Henri IV and Marie de Medici and father to Louis XIV.

Louis XIV   King of France (1643–1715) son of Louis XIII and Anne of Austria.

Luynes, Charles d'Albert, Duke of   favourite of the young Louis XIII, principal minister following the assassination of Concini in 1617 until his death in battle in 1621.

Maria-Theresa   daughter of King Philip IV of Spain and wife of Louis XIV from 1660. Marriage arranged as part of the settlement of the Peace of the Pyrenees.

Marie de Medici   wife of Henri IV and mother to Louis XIII, headed regency government during her son's minority, 1610–14, remained an important political force at court until her exile in 1630.

Marillac, Michel de   Keeper of the Seals, who favoured reform over foreign war as a priority. Political foe to Richelieu, disgraced after the Day of the Dupes in 1630.

Mazarin, Jules, Cardinal   successor to Richelieu as principal minister in December 1642 until his death in 1661. Leading figure of the regency government and during the Fronde. Target of much political opposition.

Nevers, Charles of Gonzaga, Duke of   French nobleman, succeeded to the Italian duchy of Mantua sparking fighting between France and Spain in 1629.

Retz, Jean-François Paul de Gondi, Cardinal of   Archbishop of Paris from 1653. Avowed enemy of Mazarin and leading frondeur.

Richelieu, Armand-Jean Duplessis, Cardinal   principal minister to Louis XIII from 1624 to 1642.

Saint-Cyran   Abbot, advocate of Jansenism in France, arrested on Richelieu's orders in 1638.

Séguier, Pierre   Keeper of the Seals, then Chancellor in 1635. Influential figure, very close to Richelieu, marginalised somewhat under Mazarin.

Servien, Abel   Secretary of State for War in 1630. Forced into exile by the frondeurs in 1651, named Superintendent of Finance (with Fouquet) upon his return in 1653 until his death in 1659.

Sourdis, Henri d'Escoubleau de   client of Richelieu, responsible for building palace at town of Richelieu. Archbishop of Bordeaux and commander of the Atlantic fleet. Disgraced by Richelieu following defeat in 1638.

Sully, Maximilien de Béthune, Duke of   Huguenot, minister-favourite of Henri IV. Credited with bringing the finances of the kingdom under control. Quickly fell from power after Henri IV's death in 1610.

Turenne, Henri de la Tour, Viscount of   celebrated French general, briefly joined the Fronde against the government from 1649–51, remained important military leader beyond 1661.

Vendôme, César de Bourbon, Duke of   illegitimate son of Henri IV, half-brother to Louis XIII. Ostracised by Richelieu, he re-emerged after 1642 as a key noble figure.

FURTHER READING

The secondary literature on this period is vast, so all that can be offered here is a very brief, indicative selection of some of the more recent or influential works relating to the themes addressed in this book. An effort has been made to restrict the list to English sources, except when the exclusion of a work on this basis seemed too artificial. Students are advised to rely on the bibliographies and notes of the following works for further reading in English and French.

There are a number of good introductions to the period. The most recent is David J. Sturdy (2004) *Richelieu and Mazarin: A Study in Statesmanship*, Basingstoke: Palgrave. First published in 1977, Robin Briggs (1998) *Early Modern France, 1560–1715*, 2nd ed. Oxford: Oxford University Press, has not lost any of its authority. James B. Collins (1995) *The State in Early Modern France*, Cambridge: Cambridge University Press, is strong on the late seventeenth and eighteenth centuries, but has much to say about the earlier period and can be used as a reference work on the structure and workings of government. As the title suggests, students can find a social perspective in Sharon Kettering (2001) *French Society, 1589–1715*, Harlow: Pearson. For a French perspective, students are referred to Emmanuel Le Roy Ladurie (1996) *The Ancien Regime: A History of France, 1610–1774*, trans. Mark Greengrass, Oxford: Blackwell, though it ranges widely, and often quite far, from the early seventeenth century. More useful in this regard is Yves-Marie Bercé (1992) *The Birth of Absolutism: A History of France, 1598–1661*, trans. Richard Rex, New York: St Martin's Press. A useful collection of essays with a broad coverage can be found in Mack P. Holt (ed.) (1991) *Society and Institutions in Early Modern France*, Athens: University of Georgia Press.

On Louis XIV, there is, of course, an enormous body of writing. A good point of departure for students is the recent David J. Sturdy (1998), *Louis XIV*, Basingstoke: Palgrave. Two stimulating, though conflicting, interpretations of the nature of royal authority can be found in Nicholas Henshall (1992) *The Myth of Absolutism*, London: Longman, and the older David Parker (1983) *The Making of French Absolutism*, London: Arnold. For a fuller, more recent treatment by him, see David Parker (1996) *Class and State in Ancien Régime France: The Road to Modernity?*, London: Routledge. Much of the writing on this period has been influenced by the work of J. Russell Major which stresses the representative and co-operative nature of government over traditional conceptions of absolutism. See his (1980) *Representative Government in Early Modern France*, New Haven: Yale University Press, and more recently, (1994) *From Renaissance Monarchy to Absolute Monarchy: French Kings, Nobles, and Estates*, Baltimore: Johns Hopkins University Press. Roger Mettam (1988) *Power and Faction in the France of Louis XIV*, Oxford: Blackwell, is especially important because it exposes the personal nature of political authority. Though it covers the late seventeenth century, it is based on a sensitive understanding of earlier patterns of government. Similarly, William Beik's very influential (1985) *Absolutism and Society in Seventeenth-Century France: State, Power and Provincial Aristocracy in Languedoc*, Cambridge: Cambridge University Press, focuses on the late century but has invaluable things to say about the interdependence of central and regional power over the whole century. Richard Bonney's many important writings on the period are based on much detailed research into institutional and financial history. Fortunately, there is now a collection of his principal essays, (1995) *The Limits of Absolutism in Ancien Régime France*, Aldershot: Variorum.

EARLY BOURBON MONARCHY

There can be no attempt here to provide a bibliography of the Wars of Religion (1562–1598) though a useful introduction, with a good bibliography, is R. J. Knecht (2000) *The French Civil Wars, 1562–1598*, Harlow: Pearson. For coverage which includes the wars of the early seventeenth century, see Mack P. Holt (1995) *The French Wars of Religion, 1562–1629*, Cambridge: Cambridge University Press, which also takes a more social perspective. Linking the wars with the themes of this study is Mark Greengrass (1995) *France in the Age of Henri IV*, 2nd ed., London: Longman. On Henri IV himself, students can still consult with profit David Buisseret (1984) *Henri IV: King of France*, London: Unwin Hyman. Though its coverage ends early, the conclusions in Ronald S. Love (2001) *Blood and Religion: The Conscience of Henri IV, 1553–1593*, Montreal: McGill-Queens Press, are relevant. The best coverage of Sully is Bernard Barbiche and Ségolène de Dainville-Barbiche (1997) *Sully*, Paris: Fayard. For Concini, Hélène Duccini (1991) *Concini: grandeur et misère du favori de Marie de Médici*, Paris: A. Michel. For the Edict of Nantes and its enforcement after 1598, there are a number of recent works though a good starting point is still Nicola Sutherland (1988) 'The Crown, the Huguenots and the Edict of Nantes' in M. Golden (ed.), *The Huguenot Connection*, Dordrecht: Kluwer.

LOUIS XIII AND RICHELIEU

Essential reading is the influential work by Richard Bonney (1978) *Political Change in France under Richelieu and Mazarin, 1624–61*, Oxford: Oxford University Press. On the period of Louis XIII and Richelieu more exclusively, there is a good collection of essays in Joseph Bergin and Laurence Brockliss (eds) (1992) *Richelieu and His Age*, Oxford: Oxford University Press. For the person of Louis XIII see A. Lloyd Moote (1989) *Louis XIII: The Just*, Berkeley: University of California Press. On Richelieu, there is an accessible introduction by R. J. Knecht (2000) *Richelieu*, 2nd ed., Harlow: Longman. Two of the most important studies of Richelieu's career are Joseph Bergin (1991) *The Rise of Richelieu*, New Haven: Yale University Press, and (1985) *Cardinal Richelieu: Power and the Pursuit of Wealth*, New Haven: Yale University Press. Also see the essays in Roland Mousnier (ed.) (1987) *Richelieu et la culture*, Paris: CNRS. A new, English translation is available of the older Victor L. Tapié (1984) *France in the Age of Richelieu and Louis XIII*, D. McN. Lockie (trans.), Cambridge: Cambridge University Press, which is especially good on the international context.

RELIGION

On religion and the church, the work of Joseph Bergin is essential. See his comprehensive (1996) *The Making of the French Episcopate, 1589–1661*, New Haven: Yale University Press, and (1987) *Cardinal de La Rochefoucauld: Leadership and Reform in the French Church*, New Haven: Yale University Press. Important new work can be found in Alison Forrestal (2004) *Fathers, Pastors and Kings*, Manchester: Manchester University Press. From a different perspective see Henry Phillips (1997) *Church and Culture in Seventeenth-Century France*, Cambridge, Cambridge University Press. On the Huguenots, Ray Mentzer and Andrew Spicer (eds) (2002) *Society and Culture in the Huguenot World, 1559–1685*, Cambridge: Cambridge University Press, has important essays. Philip Benedict (2001) *The Faith and Fortunes of France's Huguenots, 1600–85*, Aldershot: Ashgate, gives the Huguenots of the seventeenth century the attention they deserve, as does Elisabeth Labrousse (1985) 'Calvinism in France, 1598–1685' in M. Prestwich (ed.), *International Calvinism*, Oxford: Clarendon Press. On Jansenism, see William Doyle (1999) *Jansenism: Catholic Resistance to Authority from the Reformation to the French Revolution*, Basingstoke: Macmillan, or the older, but more focused on the early seventeenth century, A. C. Sedgewick (1977) *Jansenism in Seventeenth-Century France*, Charlottesville: University Press of Virginia. For Counter-Reformation culture see R. and S. Pillorget (1995) *France Baroque, France Classique, 1589–1715*, 2 vols, Paris: Laffont.

WAR

On the military, students should read the wide-ranging study by John Lynn (1997) *The Giant of the Grand Siècle: The French Army, 1610–1715*, Cambridge: Cambridge University Press, along with David Parrott (2001) *Richelieu's Army: War, Government and Society in France, 1624–1642*, Cambridge: Cambridge University Press. Although it deals with the late seventeenth century, Guy Rowlands (2002) *The Dynastic State and the Army under Louis XIV: Royal Service and Private Interest, 1661–1701*, Cambridge: Cambridge University Press, has very important things to say about the army and about French society generally. On the navy, see Alan James (2004) *The Navy and Government in Early Modern France, 1572–1661*, Woodbridge: Boydell. All of the above should be considered alongside Joel Cornette (1993) *Le Roi de guerre: essai sur la souveraineté dans la France du grand siècle*, Paris: Payot. For the international context of military developments and the historiographical debate on the Military Revolution, students might want to consult Clifford J. Rogers (ed.) (1995) *The Military Revolution Debate: Readings on the Military Transformation of Early Modern Europe*, Boulder: Westview. Good coverage of the complex Thirty Years' War can be found in Ronald G. Asch (1997) *The Thirty Years' War: The Holy Roman Empire and Europe, 1618–1648*, Basingstoke: Macmillan. More generally, Thomas Munck (1990) *Seventeenth-Century Europe: State, Conflict and the Social Order in Europe, 1598–1700*, Basingstoke: Macmillan is also useful.

GOVERNMENT

On rebellions, a good starting point is William Beik (1997) *Urban Protest in Seventeenth-Century France: The Culture of Retribution*, Cambridge: Cambridge University Press. See also Yves-Marie Bercé (1990) *History of Peasant Revolts: The Social Origins of Rebellion in Early Modern France*, trans. Amanda Whitmore, Cambridge: Polity, and for noble rebellion Robin Briggs (1990) 'Noble conspiracy and revolt in France, 1610–60', *Seventeenth-Century French Studies*, 12, pp. 158–76. Financial matters are at the heart of studies of the absolutist state. An excellent starting point is Richard Bonney (1998) 'What's New about the New French Fiscal History?', *Journal of Modern History* 70, 3, pp. 639–67, also see his important (1981) *The King's Debts:*

Finance and Politics in France, 1589–1661, Oxford: Clarendon Press, and James B. Collins (1988) *The Fiscal Limits of Absolutism: Direct Taxation in Early Seventeenth-Century France*, Berkeley: University of California Press. Also see Daniel Hickey (1986) *The Coming of French Absolutism: The Struggle for Tax Reform in the Province of Dauphiné, 1540–1640*, Toronto: University of Toronto Press. In addition to the work on the private fortunes of Richelieu and Mazarin, the detailed investigation of the world of financiers by Françoise Bayard (1988) *Le Monde des financiers au XVIIe siècle*, Paris: Flammarion, and Daniel Dessert (1984) *Argent, pouvoir et société au grand siècle*, Paris: Fayard, are very important. More accessible and equally important is Daniel Dessert (1987) *Fouquet*, Paris: Fayard. On the difficult relations between the government and the parlements after the Fronde see A. Hamscher (1987) *The Conseil Privé and the Parlements in the Age of Louis XIV: A Study in French Absolutism*, Philadelphia: American Philosophical Society, and especially his (1976) *The Parlement of Paris after the Fronde, 1653–1673*, Pittsburgh: University of Pittsburgh Press. An alternative perspective which should not be ignored, though it deals mainly with the late seventeenth century, is provided by John J. Hurt (2002) *Louis XIV and the Parlements: The Assertion of Royal Authority*, Manchester: Manchester University Press.

MAZARIN AND THE FRONDE

A good starting point is Orest Ranum (1993) *The Fronde: A French Revolution*, New York: Norton, which should be read along with Richard Bonney (1980) 'The English and French Civil Wars', *History*, 65, pp. 365–82. An interesting and accessible account is provided by Wendy Gibson (1998) *A Tragic Farce: The Fronde (1648–1653)*, Exeter: Elm Bank Publications. A fascinating study of the language and imagery used during the Fronde is in Christian Jouhaud (1985) *Les Mazarinades: la Fronde des mots*, Paris: Aubier. On religion, politics and the Fronde see D. A. Watts (1980) *Cardinal de Retz: The Ambiguities of a Seventeenth-Century Mind*, Oxford: Clarendon Press, and Richard M. Golden (1981) *The Godly Rebellion: Parisian Curés and the Religious Fronde, 1652–62*, Chapel Hill: University of North Carolina Press. On Mazarin, see Geoffrey Treasure (1997) *Mazarin: The Crisis of Absolutism in France*, London: Routledge. On the important matter of his finances see, in French, Claude Dulong (1999) *Mazarin*, Paris: Perrin, his (1990) *La Fortune de Mazarin*, Paris: Perrin, and G. Bordonove (1996) *Mazarin: le pouvoir et l'argent*, Paris: Pygmalion. For a different perspective on his career, Derek Croxton (1999) *Peacemaking in Early Modern Europe: Cardinal Mazarin and the Congress of Westphalia, 1643–48*, London: Associated University Presses, and Georges Dethan (1981) *Mazarin, un homme de paix à l'age baroque*, Paris: Imprimerie Nationale. A good treatment of the early Fronde is in A. Lloyd Moote (1971) *The Revolt of the Judges: The Parlement of Paris and the Fronde, 1643–52*, Princeton: Princeton University Press. Other, biographical approaches to the Fronde are offered in C. Bouyer (1999) *Gaston d'Orléans 1608–1660: séducteur, frondeur et mécène*, Paris: Albin Michel, and Ruth Kleinman (1985) *Anne of Austria: Queen of France*, Columbus: Ohio State University Press.

SOCIAL ORDER

On the social structure of France and the nobility in particular, a good recent introduction is Donna Bohanan (2001) *Crown and Nobility in Early Modern France*,

Basingstoke: Palgrave. Jonathan Dewald's excellent work on the French nobility informs his broader (1996) *The European Nobility, 1400–1800*, Cambridge: Cambridge University Press, and see his (1993) *Aristocratic Experience and the Origins of Modern Culture: France, 1570–1715*, Berkeley: University of California Press. For some valuable essays on the nobility see Ronald Asch and Adolf Birk (eds) (1991) *Princes, Patronage and the Nobility*, Oxford: Oxford University Press, and in particular Roger Mettam (1995) 'The French Nobility, 1610–1715' in H. M. Scott (ed.) *The European Nobilities in the Seventeenth and Eighteenth Centuries*, London: Longman. For a good insight into the practical workings of noble power see Sharon Kettering (1986) *Patrons, Brokers and Clients in Seventeenth-Century France*, Oxford: Oxford University Press and her other works. A useful collection is Michael Wolfe (1997) *Changing Identities in Early Modern France*, Durham: Duke University Press. Somewhat older, but still with some useful essays is Raymond F. Kierstead (ed.) (1975) *State and Society in Seventeenth-Century France*, New York: New Viewpoints. On the importance of governors, Robert Harding (1978) *Anatomy of a Power Elite: The Provincial Governors of Reformation France, 1542–1635*, New Haven: Yale University Press. On the cultural aspects of nobility, Jay M. Smith (1996) *The Culture of Merit: Nobility, Royal Service, and the Making of Absolute Monarchy in France, 1600–1789*, Ann Arbor, Michigan: University of Michigan Press and Arlette Jouanna (1989) *Le Devoir de révolte: la noblesse française et la gestation de l'état moderne, 1559–1661*, Paris: Fayard. Also important is Ellery Schalk (1986) *From Valor to Pedigree: Ideas of Nobility in France in the Sixteenth and Seventeenth Centuries*, Princeton: Princeton University Press. On the notions of kingship, a good place to start is Adrianna E. Bakos (1997) *Images of Kingship in Early Modern France: Louis XI in Political Thought, 1560–1789*, New York: Routledge. For a literary and cultural approach to the representation of the wedding of Louis XIV and Maria-Theresa, Abby E. Zanger (1997) *Scenes from the Marriage of Louis XIV: Nuptial Fictions and the Making of Absolutist Power*, Stanford, California: Stanford University Press. On towns, in addition to Beik cited above, see Philip Benedict (ed.) (1989) *Cities and Social Change in Early Modern France*, London: Unwin Hyman, especially the introduction. And more recently, Annette Finley-Croswhite (1999) *Henri IV and the Towns*, Cambridge: Cambridge University Press. A good introduction to the countryside is provided by J. Michael Hayden (1991) 'Rural Resistance to Central Authority in Seventeenth-Century France', *Canadian Journal of History*, 26, pp. 7–20. See also P. T. Hoffman (1996) *Growth in a Traditional Society: the French Countryside 1450–1815*, Princeton: Princeton University Press, and Pierre Goubert (1986) *The French Peasantry in the Seventeenth Century*, Ian Patterson (trans.), Cambridge: Cambridge University Press.

PRIMARY SOURCES

There are a number of printed, primary sources for students of this period, though most are in French. Given the deeply personal nature of seventeenth-century political authority, the best sources are the private papers of key individuals. There was no system of archiving, so official government documents were often kept among these papers. See, most prominently: Henri IV (1843–76) *Recueil des lettres missives de Henri IV* , Berger de Xivery (ed.), Paris: Imprimerie Royale. Maximilien de Béthune, duc de Sully (1988) *Les oeconomies royales de Sully*, David Buisseret and Bernard Barbiche (eds), Paris: Klincksieck. There are two collections of Richelieu's letters: Richelieu, Armand-Jean du Plessis (1975–85) *Les Papiers de Richelieu*, Pierre Grillon (ed.), Paris: Pedone. This has not entirely superseded the earlier, Richelieu (1853–77) *Lettres instructions diplomatiques et papiers d'état du cardinal de Richelieu*, M. Avenel (ed.), Paris: Imprimerie Impériale. See also a reprint of his memoirs: Richelieu (2001) *Mémoires du Cardinal de Richelieu sur le règne de Louis XIII*, Clermont Ferrand: Paleo. Also important is Henri de Sourdis (1839) *Correspondance de Henri d'Escoubleau de Sourdis*, Eugène Sue (ed.), Paris: Crapelet. For Mazarin, see Jules Mazarin (1877–1906) *Lettres du Cardinal Mazarin*, Pierre-Adolphe Chéruel and Georges d'Avenel (eds), Paris: Imprimerie Nationale.

In English, there are a number of political writings, most notably the heavily edited version of Richelieu (1961) *The Political Testament of Cardinal Richelieu*, Henry Bertram Hill (trans.), Madison: University of Wisconsin Press. See also Charles Loyseau (1994) *A Treatise of Orders and Plain Dignities*, Howell A. Lloyd (ed.), Cambridge: Cambridge University Press, and Jean Bodin (1962) *The Six Bookes of a Commonweale*, Kenneth Douglas McRae (ed.), Cambridge: Harvard University Press, and J. H. Franklin (ed.) (1969) *Constitutionalism and Resistance in the Sixteenth Century: Three Treatises by Hotman, Beza, and Mornay*, New York: Pegasus. See also J. Lough (ed.) (1985) *France Observed in the Seventeenth Century by British Travellers*, Stockfield: Oriel. Selected documents are also available in Richard Bonney (ed.) (1988) *Society and Government in France under Richelieu and Mazarin, 1624–1661*, Basingstoke: Macmillan, and W. F. Church (ed.) (1969) *The Impact of Absolutism in France: National Experience under Richelieu, Mazarin and Louis XIV*, New York: Wiley. O. and P. Ranum (eds) (1972) *The Century of Louis XIV*, New York: Walker, has a section which covers the Fronde. Roland Mousnier (1973) *The Assassination of Henry IV. The Tyrannicide Problem and the Consolidation of the French Absolute Monarchy in the Early Seventeenth Century*, Joan Spencer (trans.), London: Faber, has useful appendices, as does J. J. Shennan (ed.) (1969) *Government and Society in France, 1461–1661*, London: George Allen and Unwin.

REFERENCES

Aristide, Isabelle (1989) *La Fortune de Sully*. Paris: Comité pour l'histoire économique et financière de la France.

Bannister, Mark (2000) *Condé in Context: Ideological Change in Seventeenth-Century France*. Oxford: Legenda.

Beik, William (1997) *Urban Protest in Seventeenth-Century France: The Culture of Retribution*. Cambridge: Cambridge University Press.

Benedict, Philip (2001) *The Faith and Fortunes of France's Huguenots, 1600–1685*. Aldershot: Ashgate.

Bergin, Joseph (1999) 'The Counter-Reformation Church and Its Bishops', *Past and Present*, 165, pp. 30–73.

Bergin, Joseph (1992) 'Richelieu and His Bishops?', in J. Bergin and L. W. B. Brockliss (eds), *Richelieu and His Age*. Oxford: Clarendon Press.

Bergin, Joseph (1985) *Cardinal Richelieu: Power and the Pursuit of Wealth*. New Haven: Yale University Press.

Bonney, Richard (1996) 'The Fouquet-Colbert Rivalry and the "Revolution" of 1661', in K. Cameron and E. Woodrough (eds), *Ethics and Politics in Seventeenth-Century France*. Exeter: University of Exeter Press.

Bonney, Richard (1991) *The European Dynastic States, 1494–1660*. Oxford: Oxford University Press.

Bonney, Richard (1989) 'Was there a Bourbon Style of Government?', in K. Cameron (ed.), *From Valois to Bourbon: Dynasty, State and Society in Early Modern France*. Exeter: University of Exeter.

Bonney, Richard (1980) 'The English and French Civil Wars', *History*, 65, 365–82.

Burke, Peter (1992) *The Fabrication of Louis XIV*. New Haven: Yale University Press.

Burke, Peter (1992) 'The Languages of Orders in Early Modern Europe', in M. L. Bush (ed.) *Social Orders and Social Classes in Europe since 1500*. London: Longman.

Church, William F. (1972) *Richelieu and Reason of State*. Princeton: Princeton University Press.

Collins, James B. (1995) *The State in Early Modern France*. Cambridge: Cambridge University Press.

Desplat, Christian (1991) 'Louis XIII and the Union of Béarn to France', in Mark Greengrass (ed.), *Conquest and Coalescence: The Shaping of the State in Early Modern Europe*. London: Arnold.

Dessert, Daniel (1995) 'La Marine royale, une filiale Colbert', in Charles Giry-Delaison and R. Mettam (eds), *Patronages et clientèlismes, 1550–1750*. London, Institut Français.

Dessert, Daniel (1987) *Fouquet*. Paris: Fayard.

Dessert, Daniel (1984) *Argent, pouvoir et société au grand siècle*. Paris: Fayard.

Diefendorf, Barbara (2001) 'Contradictions of the Century of Saints: Aristocratic Patronage and the Convents of Counter Reformation Paris', *French Historical Studies*, 24, 3, pp. 469–99.

Doolin, Paul Rice (1935) *The Fronde*. Cambridge: Harvard University Press.

Doyle, William (1996) *Venality: The Sale of Offices in Eighteenth-Century France*. Oxford: Clarendon Press.

Elliott, J. H. and L. W. B. Brockliss (eds) (1999) *The World of the Favourite*. New Haven: Yale University Press.

Elliott, J. H. (1991) *Richelieu and Olivares*, 2nd ed. Cambridge: Cambridge University Press.

Golden, Richard M. (1981) *The Godly Rebellion: Parisian Curés and the Religious Fronde, 1652–1662*. Chapel Hill, N.C.: University of North Carolina Press.

Greengrass, Mark (1995) *France in the Age of Henri IV*, 2nd ed. London: Longman.

Hamscher, A. (1976) *The Parlement of Paris after the Fronde, 1653–1673*. Pittsburgh: University of Pittsburgh Press.

Hayden, J. Michael (1974) *France and the Estates General of 1614*. Cambridge: Cambridge University Press.

Henshall, Nicholas (1992) *The Myth of Absolutism*. London: Longman.

James, Alan (2002) 'Huguenot Militancy and the Seventeenth-Century Wars of Religion', in R. Mentzer and A. Spicer (eds), *Society and Culture in the Huguenot World, 1559–1685*. Cambridge: Cambridge University Press.

Kossmann, Ernst H. (1954) *La Fronde*. Leiden: Universitaire Pers Leiden.

Love, Ronald S. (2001) *Blood and Religion: The Conscience of Henri IV, 1553–1593*. Montréal: McGill-Queens University Press.

Love, Ronald S. (1996) 'Rituals of Majesty: France, Siam, and Court Spectacle in Royal Image Building at Versailles in 1685 and 1686', *Canadian Journal of History*, 31, 171–98.

Madelin, Louis (1931) *La Fronde*. Paris: Plon.

Mettam, Roger (1988) *Power and Faction in the France of Louis XIV*. Oxford: Blackwell.

Moote, A. Lloyd (1989) *Louis XIII: The Just*. Berkeley: University of California Press.

Moote, A. Lloyd (1971) *The Revolt of the Judges: The Parlement of Paris and the Fronde, 1643–52*. Princeton: Princeton University Press.

Mousnier, Roland (1971) *Peasant Uprisings in Seventeenth-Century France, Russia, and China*, trans. Brian Pearce. London: Allen and Unwin.

Parker, David (1983) *La Rochelle and the French Monarchy: Conflict and Order in 17th Century France*. Woodbridge: Boydell.

Parrott, David (2001) *Richelieu's Army: War, Government, and Society in France, 1624–1642*. Cambridge: Cambridge University Press.

Parrott, David (1992) 'Richelieu and "les grands"', in J. Bergin and L. W. B. Brockliss (eds), *Richelieu and His Age*. Oxford: Clarendon Press.

Porchnev, Boris (1963) *Les Soulèvements populaires en France de 1623 à 1648*. Paris: SEVPEN.

Ranum, Orest (1993) *The Fronde: A French Revolution*. New York: Norton.

Rapley, Elizabeth (1990) *The Dévotes: Women and Church in Seventeenth-Century France*. Montréal: McGill-Queens University Press.

Roberts, Penny (2004) 'Royal Authority and Justice during the French Religious Wars', *Past and Present*, 184, pp. 3–32.

Rowlands, Guy (2002) *The Dynastic State and the Army under Louis XIV: Royal Service and Private Interest, 1661–1701*. Cambridge: Cambridge University Press.

Rule, John C. (1969) 'Louis XIV, Roi-Bureaucrate', in J. C. Rule (ed.), *Louis XIV and the Craft of Kingship*. Ohio: Ohio State University Press.

Salmon, J. H. M. (1981) 'Storm over the Noblesse', *Journal of Modern History*, 53, 242–57.

Sturdy, David J. (2004) *Richelieu and Mazarin*. Basingstoke: Palgrave.

Weber, Herman (1992) ' "Une Bonne Paix": Richelieu's Foreign Policy and the Peace of Christendom', in J. Bergin and L. W. B. Brockliss (eds), *Richelieu and His Age*. Oxford: Clarendon Press.

Westrich, Sal (1972) *The Ormée of Bordeaux: A Revolution during the Fronde*. Baltimore: Johns Hopkins University Press.

GLOSSARY

Bailliage   the smallest administrative unit or financial district in France. Referred to as *sénéchaussées* in southern France and Brittany.

Brevets   additional articles to a formal edict which do not carry the same legal weight.

Bureau de Finances   a body of Treasurers-General with responsibility for tax collection in a given area.

Chambre de Justice   an occasional investigation into the dealings of financiers or financial officers with the purpose of punishing corruption and peculation.

Chambre St Louis   the meeting place where the demands of the leaders of the early stages of the Fronde were drafted.

Counter Reformation   a convenient, short-hand term to refer to the whole process of Catholic Reform in the sixteenth and seventeenth centuries and all of the cultural and artistic developments associated with the resurgent church.

Creature   a term willingly accepted by people who owed their political position to the influence and patronage of someone else. People felt themselves, literally, to be the political creation of others.

Dévots   the name given to the people at court who felt a particular responsibility to the church in Rome and who felt that the interest of Christendom and of the church should come before those of the state.

Élu   a financial officer, whose jurisdiction was called an *éléction*, with responsibility for ensuring the collection of taxes on behalf of the crown in those regions that did not have provincial estates.

Estates-General   the main representative body in France which included representatives from the three main orders in society: the clergy, the nobility, and the 'third' estate. Though it represented the interests of the country at large, it met at the request of the crown and only once in the seventeenth century.

Fronde   a period of prolonged civil resistance and armed struggle against the government from 1648 to 1653 which involved people from different parts of society and covered most of the country.

Gabelle   a salt tax, making it one of the most important sources of tax revenue. Those who collected it were called *gabeleurs* and were often disliked.

Gallicanism   an ideological position or tendency which favoured the relative independence of the French church from Rome.

Grand Siècle   literally, great century, a golden age.

Hôtel de Ville   the seat of municipal government, or city hall.

Huguenots   the name given to the French Protestant minority.

Intendant a commissioner directly appointed by the crown with wide-ranging powers to enforce royal authority either in a given province or, in the case of the *intendants d'armées*, a given army.

Jansenism a religious movement within the Catholic church that was eventually declared heretical for a superficial resemblance to Calvinism, its individualism and for its opposition to the Jesuits.

Lit de Justice a legal process by which a king, attending in person, could force the registration of an edict by a reluctant parlement.

Livre the basic unit of French currency.

Mazarinades a series of pamphlets and posters which mounted a vicious political attack on Cardinal Mazarin and the government during the Fronde.

Ormée the name assumed by the short-lived, radical municipal government that seized power in Bordeaux during the Fronde.

Parlement a judicial body which acted as a high court and as a legal custodian, registering and enforcing laws issued by the crown. The parlement of Paris was the largest, and most prestigious, with a jurisdiction over nearly two thirds of the country, though some provinces had their own parlement. Not to be confused with the English legislative 'parliament'.

Paulette a voluntary annual fee that guaranteed the right to bequeath an office to an heir.

Pays d'État a province with a provincial estates, which could be convened for the purposes of raising local taxes or airing local grievances. A *pays d'état* had more autonomy than a *pays d'éléction*, where the collection of taxes was more directly the business of the central government.

Prince of the blood a nobleman with the particular distinction of being related to the king and having a claim to the throne.

Regency a period of government when control of government was assumed by someone else during a king's minority, usually the Queen Mother.

Rentes a bond issued by the government that was guaranteed against a given government revenue, often municipal taxes.

Robe nobility so-called after the robes worn by judges to denote a nobility conferred through administrative service to the crown. 'Robe nobles' had difficulty attaining the status and influence of 'sword nobles' who often resented them for their pretensions.

Sorbonne the faculty of theology at the University of Paris.

Sword nobility so-called for the military service which traditionally conferred nobility. 'Sword nobles' usually had an ancient lineage and considered themselves to be more legitimate or important than others who were more recently ennobled.

Taille the main direct tax, essentially a hearth tax, though the basis on which it was calculated varied between regions.

Tax farmer someone who speculates by bidding for the opportunity to collect a given tax, or set of taxes, in the hope of exceeding the initial outlay.

Valtelline a strategic alpine pass in Switzerland, coveted by both France and Spain.

Venality the practice of selling, or auctioning, government offices for money.

INDEX

STUART BRITAIN

Social Change and Continuity: England 1550–1750 (Second edition)
Barry Coward

James I (Second edition)
S. J. Houston

The English Civil War 1640–1649
Martyn Bennett

Charles I, 1625–1640
Brian Quintrell

The English Republic 1649–1660 (Second edition)
Toby Barnard

Radical Puritans in England 1550–1660
R. J. Acheson

The Restoration and the England of Charles II (Second edition)
John Miller

The Glorious Revolution (Second edition)
John Miller

EARLY MODERN EUROPE

The Renaissance (Second edition)
Alison Brown

The Emperor Charles V
Martyn Rady

French Renaissance Monarchy: Francis I and Henry II (Second edition)
Robert Knecht

The Protestant Reformation in Europe
Andrew Johnston

The French Wars of Religion 1559–1598 (Second edition)
Robert Knecht

Philip II
Geoffrey Woodward

The Thirty Years' War
Peter Limm

Louis XIV
Peter Campbell

Spain in the Seventeenth Century
Graham Darby

Peter the Great
William Marshall

EUROPE 1789–1918

Britain and the French Revolution
Clive Emsley

Revolution and Terror in France 1789–1795 (Second edition)
D. G. Wright

Napoleon and Europe
D. G. Wright

The Abolition of Serfdom in Russia 1762–1907
David Moon

Nineteenth-Century Russia: Opposition to Autocracy
Derek Offord

The Constitutional Monarchy in France 1814–48
Pamela Pilbeam

The 1848 Revolutions (Second edition)
Peter Jones

The Italian Risorgimento
M. Clark

Bismarck & Germany 1862–1890 (Second edition)
D. G. Williamson

Imperial Germany 1890–1918
Ian Porter, Ian Armour and Roger Lockyer

The Dissolution of the Austro-Hungarian Empire 1867–1918 (Second edition)
John W. Mason

Second Empire and Commune: France 1848–1871 (Second edition)
William H. C. Smith

France 1870–1914 (Second edition)
Robert Gildea

The Scramble for Africa (Second edition)
M. E. Chamberlain

Late Imperial Russia 1890–1917
John F. Hutchinson

The First World War
Stuart Robson

Austria, Prussia and Germany 1806–1871
John Breuilly

Napoleon: Conquest, Reform and Reorganisation
Clive Emsley

The French Revolution 1787–1804
Peter Jones

The Origins of the First World War (Third edition)
Gordon Martel

The Birth of Industrial Britain
Kenneth Morgan

EUROPE SINCE 1918

The Russian Revolution (Second edition)
Anthony Wood

Lenin's Revolution: Russia 1917–1921
David Marples

Stalin and Stalinism (Third edition)
Martin McCauley

The Weimar Republic (Second edition)
John Hiden

The Inter-War Crisis 1919–1939
Richard Overy

Fascism and the Right in Europe 1919–1945
Martin Blinkhorn

Spain's Civil War (Second edition)
Harry Browne

The Third Reich (Third edition)
D. G. Williamson

The Origins of the Second World War (Second edition)
R. J. Overy

The Second World War in Europe
Paul MacKenzie

The French at War 1934–1944
Nicholas Atkin

Anti-Semitism before the Holocaust
Albert S. Lindemann

The Holocaust: The Third Reich and the Jews
David Engel

Germany from Defeat to Partition 1945–1963
D. G. Williamson

Britain and Europe since 1945
Alex May

Eastern Europe 1945–1969: From Stalinism to Stagnation
Ben Fowkes

Eastern Europe since 1970
Bülent Gökay

The Khrushchev Era 1953–1964
Martin McCauley

The European Union since 1945
Alasdair Blair

Hitler and the Rise of the Nazi Party
Frank McDonough

The Soviet Union Under Brezhnev
William Tompson

NINETEENTH-CENTURY BRITAIN

Britain before the Reform Acts: Politics and Society 1815–1832
Eric J. Evans

Parliamentary Reform in Britain c. 1770–1918
Eric J. Evans

Democracy and Reform 1815–1885
D. G. Wright

Poverty and Poor Law Reform in Nineteenth-Century Britain
1834–1914: From Chadwick to Booth
David Englander

The Birth of Industrial Britain: Economic Change 1750–1850
Kenneth Morgan

Chartism (Third edition)
Edward Royle

Peel and the Conservative Party 1830–1850
Paul Adelman

Gladstone, Disraeli and later Victorian Politics (Third edition)
Paul Adelman

Britain and Ireland: From Home Rule to Independence
Jeremy Smith

TWENTIETH-CENTURY BRITAIN

The Rise of the Labour Party 1880–1945 (Third edition)
Paul Adelman

The Conservative Party and British Politics 1902–1951
Stuart Ball

The Decline of the Liberal Party 1910–1931 (Second edition)
Paul Adelman

The British Women's Suffrage Campaign 1866–1928
Harold L. Smith

War & Society in Britain 1899–1948
Rex Pope

The British Economy since 1914: A Study in Decline?
Rex Pope

Unemployment in Britain between the Wars
Stephen Constantine

The Attlee Governments 1945–1951
Kevin Jefferys

The Conservative Governments 1951–1964
Andrew Boxer

Britain under Thatcher
Anthony Seldon and Daniel Collings

Britain and Empire 1880–1945
Dane Kennedy

INTERNATIONAL HISTORY

The Eastern Question 1774–1923 (Second edition)
A. L. Macfie

India 1885–1947: The Unmaking of an Empire
Ian Copland

The United States and the First World War
Jennifer D. Keene

Women and the First World War
Susan R. Grayzel

Anti-Semitism before the Holocaust
Albert S. Lindemann

The Origins of the Cold War 1941–1949 (Third edition)
Martin McCauley

Russia, America and the Cold War 1949–1991 (Second edition)
Martin McCauley

The Arab–Israeli Conflict
Kirsten E. Schulze

The United Nations since 1945: Peacekeeping and the Cold War
Norrie MacQueen

Decolonisation: The British Experience since 1945
Nicholas J. White

The Collapse of the Soviet Union
David R. Marples

WORLD HISTORY

China in Transformation 1900–1949
Colin Mackerras

Japan Faces the World 1925–1952
Mary L. Hanneman

Japan in Transformation 1952–2000
Jeff Kingston

China since 1949
Linda Benson

South Africa: The Rise and Fall of Apartheid
Nancy L. Clark and William H. Worger

Race and Empire
Jane Samson

US HISTORY

American Abolitionists
Stanley Harrold

The American Civil War 1861–1865
Reid Mitchell

America in the Progressive Era 1890–1914
Lewis L. Gould

The United States and the First World War
Jennifer D. Keene

The Truman Years 1945–1953
Mark S. Byrnes

The Korean War
Steven Hugh Lee

The Origins of the Vietnam War
Fredrik Logevall

The Vietnam War
Mitchell Hall

American Expansionism 1783–1860
Mark S. Joy

The United States and Europe in the Twentieth Century
David Ryan

The Civil Rights Movement
Bruce J. Dierenfield